THE INFLUENCE OF GESENIUS
ON HEBREW LEXICOGRAPHY

CONTRIBUTIONS TO ORIENTAL HISTORY AND PHILOLOGY
No. 11

THE
INFLUENCE OF GESENIUS
ON
HEBREW LEXICOGRAPHY

by   RxtsAP

EDWARD FREDERICK MILLER, M.A., Ph.D.

Columbia University Fellow in Semitics
1924-1925

New York
COLUMBIA UNIVERSITY PRESS
1927

TO THE MEMORY OF MY DEAR
MOTHER AND FATHER

COLUMBIA UNIVERSITY PRESS
Columbia University
New York

FOREIGN AGENT
HUMPHREY MILFORD
Amen House, E. C.
London

CONTENTS

The importance of Wilhelm Gesenius in the development of the study of the Hebrew of the Old Testament has been much greater than most students are aware of. It has extended far beyond the confines of his native land and has made his name almost synonoymous with that development. It was, therefore, proper that we should possess some account of this influence.

Mr. Miller has tried to trace this by a study of the growth of the Manual Lexicon of Gesenius; and, with much patience and with success, has made this influence clear to all students and readers. I heartily commend his work.

RICHARD GOTTHEIL.

INTRODUCTION

WILLIAM GESENIUS

Heinrich Friedrich Wilhelm Gesenius, the father of modern Hebrew lexicography, was born Feb. 3, 1786, at Nordhausen, a town of Hanover, south of the Harz Mountains. He died Oct. 23, 1842, at the age of 56. His father, Dr. Wilhelm Gesenius, was a learned physician, who left some writings on natural history and medicine.[1]

Young Gesenius received his first schooling from a private teacher Johann Ehring, who outlived him. Then he entered *Tertia* of the *Gymnasium* in his native city, where the reformer Justus Jonas, the great Orientalist J. H. Michaelis, and the eminent philologian F. A. Wolf had received their first training.[2] Here his teachers were J. C. F. Poppe and Dir. C. L. Lenz. The former died very soon after, in the year 1801, the same year in which Gesenius' father died. The elder Gesenius' death frustrated the son's plan to attend the *Gymnasium* in Gotha, since his mother refused to part with him. Dir. Lenz, in whose house he subsequently lived, and into whose charge he had been given, exercised a great influence over him. Lenz was an accomplished Latin student. He drilled his students in Latin speech, and taught the Greek and the Latin classics. "In his religion he was strict and orthodox, an enemy of all frivolity and unchurchly conduct, and, as regards the latter, especially scathing in his denunciations."[3] He noticed the promising mental faculties of the youth, who overtopped his comrades perceptibly, and was already at this time the best Hebrew student in the school."[4]

[1] Hirsch, *Biographisches Lexikon der Aerzte.*
[2] Gesenius, H., *Ein Erinnerungsblatt*, 19.
[3] *Neuer Nekrolog der Deutschen*, 1823, IX, 369.
[4] *Intelligenzblatt der ALZ*, 1842, 505.

Gesenius always cherished the memory of the institution. On October 4, 1824, he made it a gift of all his books in fine bindings, just as his predecessor Wolf had done.

In 1803, Gesenius left Nordhausen to go to the now extinct University of Helmstedt. Here he began as a student of theology. Pott, in whose house he lived, and Lichtenstein awakened in him an increased interest in Hebrew studies; while Bredow, who was a talented classical philologian and teacher, kept alive his interest in history and philology. A very noteworthy contact was made with Heinrich Henke. Henke was professor of theology at Helmstedt from 1778-1809. Cheyne says that he "appears to have been an excellent specimen of the rationalism of that day." [5] He was a classical scholar and a theologian. He wrote the *Kirchengeschichte des 18. Jahrhunderts,* 1802-1804. This history, although of some value for its presentation of the material and its illustration of special events, was tinctured too much by a subjective rationalism to have enduring value. [6] Cheyne, no doubt correctly, considered it unfortunate that Gesenius should come into contact with Henke, "because Gesenius' nature was a less devout one than his teacher's, and the young student instinctively fastened on the colder and more negative side of rationalistic thought." [7] It is, of course, hazardous to try to say just how much of his rationalism Gesenius owed to Henke; but we are quite sure that it was Henke who inspired Gesenius to exchange his future theological career for an academic one. [8]

From Helmstedt Gesenius passed on to Goettingen, where he studied under Eichhorn and Tychsen. Eichhorn, although a rationalist, did much to bring the Biblical writings back to the historical foundation which the deists had attempted to wipe out. [9] Tychsen was an authority on Jewish learning and Semitic numismatics, but lacked practical wisdom as appeared in his controversies with Kennicott. [10] Ewald had the same teachers later on.

Gesenius had begun to teach while he was still at Helmstedt, where he taught in the Paedagogium. Easter, 1806, he went to Goettingen, where he was *repetent* in the theol-

[5] Cheyne, *Founders of Old Testament Criticism,* 54.
[6] Redslob, *ADB,* XI, 755.
[7] Cheyne, *ibidem.*
[8] Kraetschmar, *Realencyclopaedie,*[3] VI, 624 f. *Intelligenzblatt,* 1842, 506.
[9] *Realencyclopaedie,*[3] V, 235.
[10] Ibidem, XII, 45 f.

ogical faculty. He later prided himself because Neander, later the great church historian, had been one of his first pupils. Primarily he lectured on philology. He announced lectures on the Odyssey, Hesiod, and Juvenal. He conducted exercises in Latin speech and disputation. In Semitics he taught Hebrew and Arabic grammar; lectured on Genesis and Psalms, and gave Introduction to the Old Testament. Heyne was opposed to the lectures on philology, and they were dropped in 1808.[11] As a rule, about thirty students attended these lectures. This was considered a good number when compared with the number in Eichhorn's classes.[12]

At Goettingen, Gesenius lectured during five semesters without the prospect of a small salary or an extraordinary professorship. In fact, Eichhorn and Heyne were not particularly anxious to keep this young scholar, who allowed himself outspoken statements concerning the late celebrities at Goettingen.[13] Gesenius was therefore compelled to accept a position at the Catholic *Gymnasium,* at Heiligenstadt, in March, 1809. While teaching here he profited from his proximity to Goettingen, where he went from time to time for materials for his Hebrew studies, which had already progressed considerably.

Through Niemeyer's influence, Gesenius was called to the theological faculty of the University at Halle, where he became extraordinary professor, February 8, 1810. His friend, Wegscheider, had just come from Rinteln to Halle as *ordinarius.* On June 16th, Gesenius was promoted to an ordinary professorship, after he had refused a promising call to Breslau. Halle was the sphere of Gesenius' subsequent academic activity. He taught there for thirty years. Only two times was Halle in danger of losing him: (1) When he was called to Goettingen, to take the place made vacant by Eichhorn's death, and (2) when he was called to Oxford in 1832, where he was to receive as many pounds sterling as he received *Thalers* in Halle.[14]

At Halle, Gesenius taught primarily in Semitics. He delivered two lectures, called *publica,* a day, and had occasional courses and private classes. His lectures were divided into a course of two years: (1) The exegetical

11 *Intelligenzblatt,* 1842, 507.
12 *Ibidem,* 506 f.
13 *Neuer Nekrolog der Deutschen,* II, 739.
14 Cheyne, *op. cit.,* 55. His authority is Benecke, *Wilhelm Vatke,* 83.

course, embracing: Genesis, Job, selected Psalms, and
Isaiah; (2) Introduction to the Old Testament, Hebrew antiquities, and Ecclesiastical history. The latter he had only
because there was no one else to take it. The church-
historian Gieseler, later at Goettingen, was one of his
pupils.[15]. At Halle he also lectured on the Minor Prophets
and the Apocalypse; explained *Hariri,* and taught Hebrew
grammar, Syriac, Aramaic, Late Hebrew, and palaeography.
The first two of these were given only once, and were
known as *publica.* Besides these lectures, Gesenius acted as
leader in a *Seminar* for students of advanced Semitic study.
Here some of the most successful professors of the Old
Testament later on, in German as well as in foreign universities, received their training. Some prominent men who
came from this school were: Peter von Bohlen; Hoffman,
later at Jena; Hupfeld, Marburg; Roediger, Halle; Tuch,
Leipzig; and Vatke and Bernary, Berlin.

Gesenius was an extremely gifted teacher and lecturer.
Although an empiricist, incapable of broad philosophical
views, he had a way of making his lectures interesting.
Haym, a student during Gesenius' later years, gives us a
graphic account of Gesenius' class-room:[17]

Finally, when the last seat has been occupied, we see the
figure, with which we had already acquainted ourselves,
ascend the platform. With what freshness and vivacity the
subject is attacked; what animation pervades the entire lecture! Outwardly loosely arranged and disconnected, the
lecture, nevertheless, is clear and logical. First critical
questions are taken up. The entire matter is spread before
us so clearly that we can follow step by step. How near
to us the critical problems approach! We imagine that we
ourselves have the task in hand, and are conducting the
critical play.

Robinson, an American scholar, who heard Gesenius, has
this to say:[18]

Gesenius was popular as a lecturer, and his lecture-room
was always thronged. His manner was easy and natural,
too often perhaps familiar, always animated, and without
any effort for effect. So clear were his own conceptions,
that he never uttered a sentence, nor scarcely ever wrote
one, which even the dullest intellect did not at once com-
prehend. In this respect he may be said to stand out almost

[15] Robinson, *Bibliotheca Sacra,* 1843, 371.
[16] *Neuer Nekrolog der Deutschen,* 1842, II, 740.
[17] R. H. S., *Wilhelm Gesenius,* Halle, 1886. A pamphlet.
[18] Robinson, *Bibliotheca Sacra,* 1843, 372.

alone among modern German scholars.

His desire to teach was so great that during the last half-year of his life, when he was quite ill, he arose from his bed to lecture, only to retire again after the lecture.[19] In his seminar, organized in 1813, he showed all the qualities of a successful leader. Here he put aside the formality which was necessary in the class-room to assume an open an easy manner with his students. He did not present finished views, but he studied with his students. He presented the materials, and the students were induced to do individual work. They were led to suppose that they were standing on their own feet, whereas actually they were supporting themselves verywhere on the master.[20]

The result was that Gesenius' classes grew amazingly. Robinson tells us that he was present at Gesenius' opening lecture on Genesis, in 1808. Gesenius was then lecturing for the tenth time on this book. Nineteen years before, when he began at Halle, he had had only fourteen students in his class, but he was satisfied because the renowned Vater had had only seven. Now he had five hundred students in this particular class. The enrollment at the university was one thousand three hundred and thirty. Of these, 944 were students of theology, drawn there for the most part by the celebrity of Gesenius. There were natives of Germany, England, Denmark, Poland, Holland, Greece, and the United States.[21] In his two classes, Gesenius had one thousand students and over. This popularity continued with little fluctuation until his death. It is alleged that after 1810 hardly one student studied theology at Halle who did not study under Gesenius.

Gesenius began to write early in life. At the University of Helmstedt he published a small glossary to an edition of Tacitus' *Germania*. At Goettingen, August 19, 1806, he published his inaugural dissertation: *Symbolae observationum in Ovidii Fastos, novae Fastorum editionis specimen.* In this he dealt more with the astronomy and religious customs of these people than with the criticism and grammar of the text. The value of the critical notes in this dissertation was recognized.[22] From now on Gesenius devoted himself almost exclusively to the study of Oriental philology and literature. His writing embraced Hebrew lexicography,

[19] *Intelligenzblatt*, 1842, 509.
[20] Haym, cf. *ALZ*, 1843, 298.
[21] Robinson, *Bibliotheca Sacra*, 1843, 366 f.
[22] *Goettinger Gelehrten Anzeigen*, 1806, 1689.

grammar, and exegesis; besides many important contributions to paleography.

Gesenius' contributions to lexicography are most important of all. He began his first lexicon[23] when he was *repentent*, at Goettingen, in the winter of 1806-1807. After Easter, 1807, he began the actual working-out of his plans, and within a year, the first volume was ready to appear. Vater, in Halle, helped him find a publisher, F. C. W. Vogel, whose concern has edited the lexicon in a laudable manner ever since. The success of Gesenius' first lexicographical attempt was immediate. This larger lexicon was soon followed by the shorter one, in 1815, [24] which was published four times in German and once in Latin, by Gesenius himself; while the larger lexicon was soon after published as a Hebrew and Chaldee-Latin Thesaurus, in 1829, and not finished till 1858, by Roediger. All of Gesenius' lexicons enjoyed great popularity; the editions of 3,000 copies of each of the Hebrew and Chaldee-German manual lexicons were quickly disposed of. We shall discuss these lexicons with more detail farther on.

Gesenius' grammatical works are of hardly less importance than his lexicographical ones. The grammar appeared a year after the lexicon had been published, as a small book of two hundred and two pages, 8vo.[25] This grammar, in its first editions, shows dependence on Schroeder, Hezel, and Vater, but its lucid manner of presentation immediately won recognition, so that it practically replaced all other grammars.[26] The grammar follows the empirical method, the same as does the lexicon. It appeared in thirteen editions during Gesenius' lifetime. Of these the tenth edition contains the greatest revision. Whereas Gesenius made use of the materials of his predecessors in the first edition, his later editions show the influence of Ewald's grammars.[27] After Gesenius' death, the 14.-21. editions were edited by E. Roediger; and the 22.- 28. by E. Kautzsch. The grammar was the most used of Gesenius' writings, and was translated into almost all of the European languages. In 1814, a Hebrew reader was published as a supplement to it.

[23] Gesenius, *Hebraeisch-deutsches Handwoerterbuch*, 1810-12.
[24] See Bibliography.
[25] Gesenius, W., *Hebraeische Grammatik*, Halle, 1813.
[26] Cf. Diestel, *Geschichte des Alten Testaments*, 566.
[27] Ewald H., *Kritische Grammatik der Hebraeischen Sprache*.

This reader went through six editions during Gesenius' lifetime.

To the grammatical works belongs also: *Die Geschichte der hebraeischen Sprache und Schrift*, 1815. This small book contains valuable grammatical and lexicographical notes, as well as an interesting account of all the work on lexicography and grammar before Gesenius. The book was hastily compiled. Gesenius wished to revise it later, but was unable to do so. Steinschneider has left a copy of this book with many valuable corrections,[28] but a new edition was never printed.

The *Lehrgebaeude der hebraeischen Sprache* was published in 1817. This work is a masterly collection of the grammatical phenomena of the Hebrew language. In it Gesenius shows more extensively the peculiarities of the younger and the older stages of the language, also of poetry and prose; and he compared other dialects besides the Arabic. To this work the objection was rightfully raised that Gesenius did not enter into the philosophy of the language sufficiently well. He made the mistake to have too many copies printed; the book sold badly; so that a new edition could not be prepared in time to keep it abreast of Gesenius' later researches. His desire to rewrite this *Lehrgebaeude* was also not granted.[29]

Closely allied to his lexicographical and grammatical works is his Commentary on the Book of Isaiah, the first part containing the translation appeared as early as 1820; the other, embracing the commentary, was published in 1821.[30] Cheyne [31] says: "In all respects this work is a mine of accurate philological and historical information up to its date. Its Biblical theology, it is true, cannot receive high praise." Gesenius was not so much an exegete as a lexicographer. His commentary lacks the religious fervor and piety which pervades, for example, the commentaries of Franz Delitzsch. Although some of the positions taken by Gesenius as to the origin of this book and its prophetic character can not be accepted by conservative Biblical

---

[28] See copy in Jewish Theological Sem. Library, New York.
[29] Robinson, *Bibliotheca Sacra*, 1840, 364 f.
[30] Gesenius, W., *Der Prophet Jesaiah* . . . 4 pts., 1820-21. In 1829, appeared a revision of the translation only.
[31] Cheyne, *Founders*, 1893, 62.
[32] e. g., Robinson, *Bibliotheca Sacra*, 365.

scholars,[32] it is not to be overlooked that Gesenius did not make as many concessions to the rationalism of his time, as is ordinarily supposed. He considered the Massoretic Text to be fairly sound (*Einleitung* of Part II, para. 8); in this, stemming the unbounded caprice of the previous period. In denying the authenticity of the Isaiah 40-66, he nevertheless opposed the fragmentists, who wanted to make many more divisions. His view of prophesy also differed from that of the extreme rationalists; he considered the poet not merely *a poet of nature*, but *a herald and watchman of this theocracy and the theocratic faith.*[33a] He also repudiated the idea that the prophesies respecting the future were merely veiled historical exhibitions of the present or even the past. We are not in agreement with Gesenius in his liberal theological views, and look upon him as a moderator between the rationalists and the new-orthodox party[33b] which was arising at that time.

The works of Gesenius discussed so far formed the basis for practically all of the best exegesis of the last century. His other writings relate primarily to paleography. We shall list them chronologically. In his: *Versuch ueber die maltesische Sprache*, 1810, begun at Heiligenstadt, he showed that the Maltese was a corrupt dialect of the Arabic. He wrote an excellent treatise entitled: *De Pentateuchi Samaritani origine*, 1815; also: *Andenken an P. J. Bruns*, in the *Krit. Journal der neuesten theologischen Literatur*, III, 2, 1815; *De Samaritanorum theologia*, 1822; *Erlaeuterungen und Parallelen zum neuen Testament*, in Rosenmueller's *Biblisch-exegetisches Repertorium*, I, 1822. He added notes to the German translation of Burkhardt's Travels, 1823-24. His other writings are: *Carmina Samaritana*, in *fasci.* I of *Anecdota orientalia*, 1824; *De inscriptione phoenicio-graeca in Cyrenaica nuper reperta*, 1825; *De Bar Alio et Bar Bahlulo*, 1839; *Palaeographische Studien ueber phoenizische u. punische Schrift*, 1835; *Disputatio de inscriptione Punica Libyca*, 1836; *Scripturae linguaeque Phoeniciae Monumenta*, 1837; and: *The Himyaritic Alphabeth* in *JRGS* of London, Vol. XI, 1841. He wrote many articles for the *Allgemeine Literaturzeitung*, whose editor he was from 1828 on, to which he contributed from 1810 till his death. He wrote also for Ersch and Gruber's *Encyclopaedie*. Some of the material

[33a] *Einleitung*, par. 5.
[33b] Cf. Cheyne, *op. cit.*, 63.

was copied abroad, on Gesenius' two important journeys:
(1) To Paris, London, and Oxford, in 1820; (2) to England
and Holland, in 1836. He also incorporated it in his magazine articles, lexica, and his commentary on Isaiah. In many
of these attempts at decipherment, Gesenius did pioneer
work. All of his articles bear the stamp of his critical astute-
ness; but not everything has stood the test of time.

It is necessary once more to allude to Gesenius' religious
views. His Commentary on Isaiah shows him to be a rationalist with conservative tendencies. Robinson, who knew
Gesenius intimately, says that "his creed, perhaps, so far as
he had any, approached most nearly to a pure deism."[34]
Gesenius, although nominally a rationalist, was not an active
partisan in the spread of rationalistic ideas. He was indif-
ferent toward theological dogma. He pursued the study and
illustration of the Old Testament not as an inspired book,
but as an ancient book of graphic history and sublime
poetry.[36] His object was philological truth, though his commentary on Isaiah and his lexica, the latter in a lesser
degree, bore a rationalistic coloring.

While at Halle, charges were preferred against Gesenius
and his colleague, Wegscheider, for speaking lightly of the
miracles of the Bible in their class-rooms. The fact that
Gesenius did this is well founded.[37] The result was that
Otto von Gerlach and Ernst Hengstenberg, of the orthodox
party, published an article: *Der Rationalismus auf der Uni-
versitaet Halle*, 1830, in the *Evangelische Kirchenzeitung*, in
which they aimed at the deposition of the two teachers from
office. The method pursued by these men, namely, their
use of college note-books and class-room anecdotes, instead
of Gesenius' published works, as evidence, called forth criticism, even from those otherwise opposed to Gesenius' religious views.[38] Altenstein, the Prusian *Kultusminister*, was
compelled to investigate the matter, and he issued the following evasive statement: "That there was no reason why
he should take steps against the denounced professors;
but that the King, who did not care to bother with theolog-

[34] Robinson, *Bibliotheca Sacra*, 1843, 374.
[35] *Ibidem*.
[36] *Ibidem*.
[37] Cheyne, *op. cit.*, 58. For the entire question see: Germann, W.,
Zur Geschichte der theologischen Professuren in Halle, Zeitschrift fuer
kirchliche Wissenschaft, 1888, 396 ff.
[38] Redslob, *op. cit.*, IX, 90.

ical systems, expected of all teachers a fitting treatment of
the subject."[39] Thereupon the matter was dropped.

Gesenius was highly esteemed for his affable character.
It was his desire to be on good terms with all those around
him. Robinson says:[40]

He was kind and social in his habits; and his manners
had much more of the gentleman and man of the world than
is usual among German professors. A stranger meeting him
in society, would never have suspected that he was a labori-
ous and eminently distinguished philologist; much less the
first Hebrew scholar of his age.

But this did not prevent Gesenius from becoming involved
in a controversy with Ewald. This began as soon as Ewald
published his grammar,[41] in which he stated principles
which differed from those of Gesenius. Ewald's method
was to explain the phenomena of Hebrew grammar by
studying their origin and historical development. He took
a broader and more philosophical view of the subject than
Gesenius, and this brought him into conflict with him.
"During his visit to Goettingen, in 1827, soon after Ewald
had put forth a bitter personal attack upon him, Gesenius
nevertheless called upon him as a literary compeer and
fellow-labourour in the same department . . . (but) . . . the
proverbial acerbity of Ewald afterwards broke out again,
and never more grossly than just before the death of Gesenius."[42] It was partly Gesenius' own fault that this occurred; for in the introduction to the 13. edition of his
grammar, he had said: "Men of intelligence and individual
judgment will understand why it is that I have spared
the disciples of the study of Hebrew the unmethodical chaos
of laws and rules which is paraded under the flag of the
'new method'." This statement probably called forth the
following tirade from Ewald in connection with his short
grammar of 1841:[43]

Since Dr. Gesenius of Halle still continues insidiously to
traduce my labors in this field, without my giving him occa-
sion to do so, may he now blame himself when I say (1) That
his grammar is still altogether unscientific, useless, super-
ficial, unsatisfactory, and misleading, while whatever it contains of truth was for the most part borrowed from my

[39] *Realencyclopaedie*, VI, 626; Gesenius, H., *Gesenius*, 26.
[40] Robinson, *op. cit.*, 373.
[41] Ewald, H., *Kritische Grammatik der Hebraeischen Sprache*, 1827.
[42] Robinson, *op. cit.*, 273.
[43] Cf. *Allgemeine Literaturzeitung*, 1842, 559.

writings: (2) that I, should he fail to understand these terse but plain words, shall speak plainer to him in the future.

Gesenius was too ill to answer this charge, and he died not so very long after. Ewald's attitude in this entire affair deserves severe criticism. It is unfortunate that these two men, whose work was really complementary, could not combine their learning in an harmonious whole instead of each going his own way.

Gesenius' amiability qualified him for the office of *Prorektor* in the university, and yet it was just this trait of his character that got him into trouble. A student had been arrested and confined for a misdemeanor. Influenced by the demonstration which the other students made, Gesenius released him. When the Prussian officers sought the student they found him at supper with Gesenius, in company with some of the others. Before the term was over, Gesenius had a successor.[44]

The steadfastness of Gesenius' character showed itself in the fortitude with which he endured much sickness and sorrow that came upon him. As early as 1820 he had to make a trip for his health, which had been impaired, no doubt by his incessant labor in his early years, when he studied late into the night. In 1833 he was so ill from a disease of the lungs that his death was feared. In 1835, several of his children died. In later years a pronounced stomach-complaint grew upon him. He was seized by attacks of pain so severe at intervals that he was almost incapacitated for work. But through it all he labored with little intermission. His trouble, which was later pronounced to be gall-stones, became very accute in the spring of 1842, when the attacks were more frequent. His end came October 23, after he had endured much pain.

The nestor of Hebrew lexicography left a sorrowing company of relatives, students, and friends, who mourned his early death. His influence had been profound in the entire field of Oriental learning. He had found the study of the Hebrew Scriptures an isolated pursuit, "repulsive from the want of scientific helps."[45] He left Hebrew an extremely live subject with its philology on almost as high a basis as that of any other ancient language.

[44] Robinson, *op. cit.*, 1843, 374.
[45] Robinson, *op. cit.*, 1843, 377.

CHAPTER I

GESENIUS' LEXICOGRAPHICAL PRINCIPLES

Gesenius defined his lexicographical principles in the first edition of his Thesaurus[1] and in his essay on: *Von den Quellen der hebraeischen Wortforschung nebst einigen Regeln und Beobachtungen ueber den Gebrauch derselben,* first published in the second edition of his Manual Lexicon.[2] This essay was improved upon in the succeeding editions, and then unfortunately dropped entirely from the 11. Edition upward. In this essay, Gesenius presents a threefold classification of the sources for Hebrew lexicography: (1) The Hebrew of the Old Testament itself; (2) the traditional knowledge of the Hebrew; and (3) the cognate languages. We shall content ourselves with a condensed discussion of the sources as Gesenius has presented them.

1. The Hebrew usage of the Old Testament itself is of primary importance for the determination of the meanings of Hebrew words. For the more frequently occurring words it is well-nigh decisive. The meanings of words that occur rarely should be derived from the context wherever possible, before having recourse to any other source. Even *hapax legomena* can frequently be explained from the connection in which they stand.

The tendencies of Gesenius' predecessors had been to disregard the Hebrew usage. Gesenius once more called attention to the fact that Hebrew, as well as any other language, has an idiom and a phraseology which are altogether its own. The provincial character of the Hebrew language may

---

[1] *Hebraeisch-deutsches Handwoerterbuch,* 1810-12.
[2] *Hebraeisches und Chaldaeisches Handwoerterbuch,* 1823. Trans. by E. Robinson, *Biblical Repository,* 1833, No. IX.

be discerned from that fact that it contains words in frequent use which are not found in any of the other cognate tongues. Such words are, for example: אדמה *earth* and: אסף *to gather*. Since a word which occurs in the Old Testament once only may also be a provincialism, it is precarious to take over a meaning at random from one of the other languages.

In spite of his insistence upon Hebrew usage, Gesenius warns against the exclusive use of the Hebrew of the Old Testament for meanings of words. Stock and Gousset[3] had tried to explain Hebrew from its manifestations in the Old Testament only, and had made many mistakes. Frequently, the Hebrew usage will not yield an explanation of rare words; and even if it should yield the meanings with tolerable accuracy, it fails in the determination of the etymology and the primary meaning. Hence Gesenius said: "A knowledge of only one limited dialect, studied without connection with the whole stock to which it belongs, can never admit of a vivid apprehension of the sense."[4]

To find the Hebrew usage, the lexicographer must make use of the best concordances. He obtains the meanings of words by proceeding from the known to the unknown. In poetry he is aided by the parallel member, but he must be careful here since the parallel member often yields only a similar or a progressive thought. In finding the Hebrew usage, the individual style of writers must be observed. Certain writings, such as the books of Ezra and Nehemiah, Job and Proverbs show a relation in style.

2. Coming now to the second source of Hebrew lexicography, the traditional knowledge, we note that Gesenius divides it as follows: the ancient versions and the Rabbinical grammars, commentaries, and lexicons.

The oldest versions, the Alexandrian, and the Chaldee,[5] are translations of the Pentateuch, and date from a time when Hebrew was still known and in use. The Alexandrian Version often gives a meaning to a Hebrew word which has been lost in later Hebrew, but is still found in the Arabic. The *Chaldee* versions present a text based on tradition

---

[3] Gousset, J., *Commentarii linguae hebr.*, 1702. Stock, Chris., *Clavis linguae sanctae V. T.*, 1717-8. Cf. Gesenius, *Geschichte der hebraeischen Sprache und Schrift*, 126.
[4] Gesenius, Lexicon, Edition 3, iv.
[5] A misnomer for Aramaic.

handed down from generation to generation in the Jewish
schools. The sense given to words in the earlier Targums
is correct to a great degree.

On the other hand, the Syriac Version is not the result
of a living tradition, but of a learned study. It displays a
grammatical knowledge of the Hebrew and an eclectic use
of the Alexandrian Version, seldom of the *Chaldee* Versions.
Jerome's Latin version is valuable since it rests on the in-
struction which he received from the learned Palestinian
Jews. Jerome also compared the Alexandrian and other
Greek versions which were then extant in greater entirety.
Gesenius placed the composition of the Samaritan Version
as late as 200 A. D. He said that it does not show the
linguistical accuracy of the Palestinian Jews, nor their critical conscientiousness in preserving the text. The immediate
Arabic versions, now extant only in fragments, are of some
value. The version by R. Saadia Gaon, Ben Asher's con-
temporary, who died ca. 942 A. D., "contains along with
the earlier tradition much also which is the result of independent thought and study, though indeed often subtle and
forced."

To the discussion of the character of the versions, Gesenius added a set of rules for the proper use of them in
Hebrew lexicography. The rules are the following:

1. Care must be taken to understand the version itself.
Since various translators made them, at different periods
of time, the characteristics of each must be carefully studied.
The younger portions of the Alexandrian Version, for example, bear evidence that the Hebrew was then not so well
understood. One reason why some of the earlier lexicographers failed in using the versions was the fact that they
copied from concordances the equivalents of the version
without determining the circumstances under which a translation was made.

2. The text of the version must be carefully restored,
where this is possible, before using it; especially that of the
Alexandrian Version which is very corrupt.

3. A traditional interpretation underlies each version.
The version's value therefore depends on its age. The Palestinian and Alexandrian versions should be compared, and
where they are found to coincide, we have evidence of a
direct tradition.

4. Versions are useful to give the usage of a word in certain passages; what they do not give, and should not be expected to give, are the root-meanings and the etymologies. Exceptions to the last rule are Aquila's and the Venetian translation (*Graecus Venetus*).

At the time when the versions are no longer made, the grammatical and lexicographical investigations of the language appear. Gesenius enumerates and criticizes the works of the oldest lexicographers.[6]

1. Saadia Gaon wrote a book on seventy difficult roots which he explained according to the Talmudic tradition.

2. Menahem ben Saruk, in the beginning of the 11. C. compiled the first complete Hebrew lexicon. In this work we find the interesting feature that the biliteral (as such he considers the עו-עי-ל״ה verbs), the triliteral, and the quadriliteral roots are all placed into separate groups.

3. Rabbi Jonah, as the Jews called him, or Abu'l Walid Merwan Ibn-Janach, according to the Arabic, who lived in the 11. C., at Cordova, wrote a *Book of Roots*, from which Kimchi later borrowed his best illustrations. Rabbi Jonah went beyond the authority of the Jewish schools, and with the help of the Talmudic and the Arabic he made conjectures of his own. In his use of the Arabic he may be regarded as a forerunner of Ed. Pococke, Bochart, and Albert Schultens. Some of his explanations, which Gesenius also adopted, Gesenius considered valuable contributions to Hebrew lexicography.

4. R. Solomon Parchon (before 1161 A. D.) is the lexicographer from whose works De Rossi extracted the most important, yet not very valuable glosses. Many of the meanings were guessed merely from the connection.

5. R. David Kimchi's works began to be published in Naples in 1490. He surpassed all his predecessors in renown and became the classical lexicographer in Hebrew. Copies of his lexicon were rare at Gesenius' time.

Gesenius considered Yarchi, Aben Esra, Kimchi, and Tanchum worthy of most consideration among the commentators. They carefully omitted what properly belongs to the lexicon when they wrote their commentaries. However, there are different grades of value in their commentaries.

---

[6] We retain Gesenius' datings which are approximately correct.

Yarchi, otherwise Abraham Ben Nathan, ca. 12. Century, is a traditional Talmudic compiler; Aben Esra is much more independent; while Kimchi is both a skilful grammarian and compiler. The value of the works of these men for lexicographical purposes depends on the sources which they used, whether Talmudic, *Chaldaic,* or Arabic, and then on their own sagacity and sound judgment. In this latter respect, Abulwalid holds first place, whereas Yarchi can properly be put last. In his essay Gesenius cites many instances where these traditional sources prove serviceable, but we cannot reproduce any of them here.

The cognate dialects are the third source for the study of Hebrew lexicography. Gesenius divided them into three classes. He said:

The Semitic stock of languages divides itself, in general, into three principal branches: (1) the *Chaldaic,* which was anciently spoken in Syria, Babylonia, and Mesopotamia, and may be subdivided into the Syriac or West Aramaic and the *Chaldaic* or East Aramaic. Besides these, we have still some remains in the dialects of the Samaritans, Sabaeans, and those of Palmyra, which also belong to the Aramaic branch. (2) The Canaanitic branch in Palestine and Phoenicia. The Hebrew of the Old Testament belongs to this, besides a few remnants of the Phoenician and Punic dialects; also the later Hebrew, or Talmudic and Rabbinic. This, however, is again mingled with the Aramaic. (3) The Arabic languages of which the Ethiopic is an early secondary branch. Both of these have half-corrupted dialects. Of the former we have the Moorish and the Maltese dialects, of the latter, the Amharic.

On the basis of this outline, Gesenius furnished a history of each one of these languages and discussed the grammatical and lexicographical treatment that had been given to each one of them. Some of this material is, of course, out-of-date. To note the additional knowledge obtained since then, the reader is referred to the scholarly article: *Semitic Languages,* in the Encyclopaedia Brittanica, by Th. Noeldeke. It is of little value for our discussion to reproduce Gesenius' views. Let it suffice to say that he knew the existence of an ancient Egyptian language only from the remains imbedded in the Greek glosses and the Coptic. He correctly suspects that Persian proper names came in at the time of the Persian domination. He surmised that the names Nabuchadrezzer and Shalmanasar are of Persian origen. Assyrian, which became more or less important for

Hebrew lexicography later on, was still unknown to him.

Gesenius' special rules with regard to the use of the dialects are the following:

1. In using the dialects it should not be overlooked that the Hebrew has its own settled idiom which seldom exactly agrees with that of the kindred dialects.

2. The Arabic, of which we know more than all the other dialects and for which we have the surest helps, deserves first place as a philological aid, in Hebrew word-study. Nevertheless it is to be noted that the Aramaic usage is often nearer the Hebrew, especially in the writers of the Silver Age.

3. Since the differences in kindred dialects often rest on a change of consonants, these permutations must be studied. These changes are sometimes regular and predominant, as the transition of the Hebrew consonants: זעץ into the Aramaic דטת or less frequent. The degree of probability in certain doubtful cases is to be determined by the greater or lesser number of instances in which this permutation of a radical usually occurs.

4. A lexicographer does well to study the analogy of significations. He should study the dialects not only for words corresponding as to form, but also as to meaning, since they help to determine and illustrate the meanings.

To these special rules to be followed in using the cognate languages, Gesenius adds some rules on lexicography in general.

1. What belongs to the lexicon should carefully be separated from what properly belongs to the grammar and commentary. Simonis' Lexicon,[7] in its first editions, is half grammar in lexicographical form. It is not necessary for a lexicon to serve as a concordance by listing every form of a verb or a noun that follows the regular conjugation or paradigm. It should specify which particular forms of any words are in use, be they of a verb or noun, and whether any modification of meaning is dependent on these differences. It is the grammarian's duty to indicate the different forms of words as they occur in general; the indication of the peculiar usage of each separate form of a word is left to the lexicographer. The lexicographer must decide the correct reading of a

---

[7] Simonis, J., *Lexicon Manuale hebr. et chald.*, Halle, 1752, 1771, 1793.

corruption in the text only when the existence of a word or form depends upon it.

2. The lexicon should contain a complete list of constructions and phrases formed with words. It is important to show which particles are construed with the different verbs. This is called the syntactical side of the lexicon.

3. The language must be treated historically, that is, the diction of the different writers must be noted. Here belong the poetical diction and the language with the later Aramaic coloring, in the writings composed in and after the exile, as well as the peculiarities of individual books.

4. With regard to variations in the text, Gesenius thinks it necessary to list the variant readings of the Samaritan text and the Hebrew manuscripts. Detail in this matter belongs to a thesaurus; in the Manual Lexicon Gesenius is content to give only the Ketib and Keri completely. Gesenius held the opinion that the Massoretic text is quite well preserved. However, he says it is clear from certain variations in parallel passages that special care was bestowed upon the exact text at a later period only. Corrections can be made in these portions with much difficulty and only on internal grounds.

5. Proper names deserve a place in the lexicon, only in so far as they were originally appellatives, and contain verbal roots which would be lost to us otherwise.

6. A lexicographer must also study Oriental antiquities. Natural history, geography and mythology, all must be taken into account in Hebrew word-study.

7. Gesenius' rule for the arrangement of significations is the following. The lexicographer should list progressively the significations of each word in the most natural order, as they may have developed themselves, and illustrate them by proper examples. In the verb this must be done in each conjugation separately.[8] This is known as the historico-logical method. First, the primary, native signification of a word is sought, and from this, in logical order, the meanings and shades of sense are deduced, as they appear in various constructions and in the usage of the writers of different ages. The lexicographer thus gives a logical and historical view of each word in all its variations of signification. This is, no doubt, the best method. It is the same method that

[8] Leo, C., A Hebrew Lexicon, 1825, vi.

was later applied to other ancient languages. In modern languages Grimm first applied it in his German lexicon, the first part of which appeared in 1854; and it is followed in the great Oxford Lexicon, whose first part was issued in 1884. It can be worked out with greater accuracy and completeness only in languages, such as English and German, whose literature covers almost the entire growth of the language. In Hebrew there are gaps in the history of every word, as we have no literature of the ancient Hebrews outside of the Old Testament, and thus it is difficult to trace the different stages of growth. In seeking this primary meaning, Gesenius did not differ from his predecessors, but they were less successful in giving the developed meanings in a natural order.

8. Gesenius advocated and made use of the alphabetical order of all the words in the lexicon intended for students. In this respect his method differs from that of all his predecessors, as no Hebrew lexicon had before been printed on this basis. He justified the alphabetical order on three grounds:

1. Many words are primitive, that is, no root of a triliteral nature can be assumed with certainty to underlie them. He considered, for example, the one-syllable particles: אוֹ - אִי - אַל to be primitives; also many substantives which denote members of the body, plants, metals, and numbers; and many one-syllable substantives, as: אִישׁ-הַר-דָּם In his first editions, Gesenius was opposed to conjectural etymologies, as for example: אָחָה for אָח and אָמָם for אָם.

2. The etymology of some Hebrew words is still so uncertain that a student would not know under which root to look for the word.

3. The necessity of having all the developments of a certain root together for comparison, can be met satisfactorily in the alphabetical arrangement, by the use of cross-references. Each word is referred to its root; and each root has a list of derivatives placed at the end of the article. In this way, Gesenius attempted to do away with the most weighty objection to the alphabetical order.

These are the lexicographical principles according to which Gesenius worked. We shall attempt to show, in the following chapter, what success he had in applying them.

CHAPTER II

THE MANUAL LEXICON WITH GESENIUS AS AUTHOR

As the bibliography shows, Gesenius edited three Hebrew lexicons. The German Manual appeared in four editions. He called later on the first Hebrew lexicon which he issued[1] the first edition of his Thesaurus[2], although it was really more of a manual lexicon. We shall consider first of all this first edition which forms the basis for the subsequent lexicons. In our consideration we shall have to refer to previous attempts at Hebrew lexicography. It is, therefore, necessary to insert here a brief sketch of the most important lexicographers before Gesenius.

From the time of Reuchlin, 1454-1511, when the study of Hebrew lexicography began in earnest among Christian scholars, till a short time after Joh. Buxtorf, Jr., died 1664, the most important Hebrew lexicons were based on Rabbinic tradition and the Vulgate. The use of other dialects for comparison and etymology, though attempted, was not approved of in this period; as may be seen also from the fact that Joh. Buxtorf's *Lexicon hebraicum et chaldaicum*, Basel, 1607, enjoyed a great popularity and went through several editions. J. Coccejus' *Lexicon et commentarius*, Leyden, 1669, was also based on traditional lines. He used of the versions only the LXX and the Targums, and employed a typical mystical interpretation. Majus, who edited the second edition, in 1687, eliminated some of Coccejus' explanations, and added many comparisons from the dialects. It remained for Alb. Schultens, 1686-1750, the renowned Arab-

---

[1] Gesenius, *Hebraeisch-deutsches Handwoerterbuch*, 1810-12.
[2] Gesenius, *Theasaurus Philologicus Criticus*, 1829-1858.

ist, to make a thorough attempt in the use of the Arabic for Hebrew lexicography. By this time the study of Hebrew was carried on not so much on a traditional as on an independent scientific basis. Schultens used the Arabic mainly for primary meanings in Hebrew. The error in his work is that he failed to use the other sources adequately. He underrated the Aramaic, neglected the versions, and offended against Hebrew usage and the context. Schultens wrote no lexicon. His lexicographical notes are imbedded in his commentaries, namely, on Job (1737) and Proverbs (1748), as well as in: *Origines Hebraeae seu Hebraeae linguae antiquissima natura et indoles ex Arabiae penetralibus revocata,* 1723; Ed. 2, 1761.

The school of Oriental learning at Halle, in Germany, flourished about the same time as the school at Leyden. In Germany the three Michaelis, Johann Heinrich, Christian Benedict, and Johann David, were successively the guiding spirits in this school. The school of Hebrew at Halle may not have displayed the profound learning of the Dutch; but the work of the Michaelis is not so complicated and one-sided. They made better use of the Aramaic, the Rabbinical notes, and the Hebrew usage in the parallel passages of the Old Testament.[3] Johann David was the most important of the three. His lexicographical notes are found in: *Supplementa ad Lexica Hebraeica,* Goettingen, 1785, completed by Tychsen after his death. Although this work lacks depth, and has too much detail, it displays great circumspection and clearness.

The most important lexicographer in the age just prior to Gesenius was Joh. Simonis, born 1698. He had been a student of the two older Michaelis, and he studied privately the writings of Schultens. He is therefore a representative of both the School at Halle and the Dutch School. He published an *Onomasticon Veteris Testamenti,* Halle, 1741. His *Lexicon manuale Hebraicum et Chaldaicum* appeared in 1752. He also prepared the second edition in 1771. As Schultens, Simonis laid altogether too much emphasis on Arabic, and, in addition, the arrangement of the lexicographical material in his lexicon was faulty. After Simonis' death the lexicon retained its popularity. It was re-edited

---

[3] Bleek, *Einleitung.* Ed. 2, 1865, 138.

by J. G. Eichhorn in 1793, with many changes and additions, notably from the works of J. D. Michaelis. Simonis' lexicon was the only one that later threatened to disturb Gesenius' supreme position, especially at the time when it was re-edited by Winer, in 1828. This brief survey enables us to understand Gesenius' references to these lexicographers, which appear in connection with the first edition of his lexicon.

In the 1810-12 Edition, Gesenius attempted to explain as many words as possible from the Hebrew usage itself. By studying the context, the parallel-passages, and the traditional knowledge, he gave to words what he considered to be their proper primary meanings. Very often he dropped the primary meanings which had been proposed by the leaders of the Dutch School and their followers in Germany.

Gesenius dropped the primary meanings that had been given to certain words that occur frequently in Hebrew. Such a word was, for example: נהר. Gesenius distinguished two roots: one, *to meditate;* the other, *to separate.* Schultens' etymological hypothesis, which he had expounded in connection with Prov. 25, 4, was that this root originally meant: *to be in commotion, to boil up, to eject with violence.* *To speak* was developed by saying that it is an ejection of the word from the mouth either by speaking or enunciating. Likewise Simonis, Ed., 1771, and Eichhorn, Ed., 1793, attempted to develop all the meanings from one primary meaning. Simonis began with: *propulit, protrusit,* as the probable fundamental meaning. Gesenius said that this development is not confirmed by either the Hebrew or Arabic usage. Schultens[4] and Michaelis[5] had endeavored to develop all the meanings of: המם from the primary meaning: *to liquefy.* Simonis and Eichhorn, who follow Schultens, began with: *to cause to liquefy,* whence they derive: *to flee, to disperse.* Schultens said that the word in Exod. 14, 24, should literally be translated: "And he liquefied the army of Egypt," that is, either by fear or consternation he made them melt. Coccejus gave as the primary meaning: *to be in agitation.* Gesenius gave it the first meaning: *to terrify.*

Gesenius altered the meanings of some of the more rare

4 *Originum* . . . 488 ff.
5 *Supple.,* 555.

Hebrew words. On the authority of the traditional knowledge, he translated: אשפחות *dung, dirt*. Simonis, Eichhorn, and Coccejus were satisfied with: *sterquilinium*. According to the context and versions, Gesenius translated:
גהר *to bow oneself*, and he compared this meaning with the
Arabic: اجهر, as Schindler. He is opposed to the primary
meaning: *to cry*, from: جهر.[6] To: פעם he gave the primary
meaning: *to strike*, and he translated the Niphal: *to be disturbed*, e. g., in spirit. Michaelis,[7] after considering all the
conjectures begins with the primary meaning: *to be full*,
from the Arab: فعم . Simonis, 1771, had given the primary
meaning: *to agitate*, whence the Niphal: *to be disturbed;*
but Eichhorn introduced Michaelis' conjecture. Gesenius
translated: ראם *buffalo*, not *antelope*, as Schultens (Job,
par. 1115) and Michaelis (Supple., par. 2212).

There are many *hapax legomena*, said Gesenius, whose
meaning is universally acknowledged to be obtainable from
the study of the Old Testament usage. As such he cited, for
example: אזל *to depart*, which is given by Coccejus; דל
door; כמה *to long for* (lit. *to pine away*), the analogous
usage of which is found in the Arabic: كلف *caligavit
oculos*. Eichhorn, 1793, translated the latter: *to desire
anxiously*, i. e., to desire so vehemently that one wastes
away, while Coccejus translated: *contabescit*.

Certain difficult words, Gesenius explained by studying
the traditional remains and the cognate languages. Some of
these words are: שלט - שוף - רשף - מרץ - חצץ. To: חעץ *Gesenius* gave the meanings: *to divide*, intrans., *to be divided*.
Eichhorn, 1793, following Schultens on Job 21, 21, began
with *celeriter progressus est*, and thence derived: *to divide*.
The latter Eichhorn correctly explained from the Arabic
analogy as a denominative of: חץ. In ancient times arrows
were used when making a division. Gesenius did not give
this analogy, although it is a good one. To: מרץ Gesenius,
following Kimchi, gave the primary meaning: *to be violent,
strong*, and said that this fits all the passages. But he also
referred to the other view that it may mean: *aegrum esse,
to be sick*, in certain passages, and: *to be sweet*, in Job 6,

---

[6] *Ibidem*, 274.
[7] *Ibidem*, 2031 f.

25 f. Due to this uncertainty of meaning, Gesenius had two
roots, while Eichhorn, 1793, had only one with the primary
meaning: *to be sick, sickly.* As Eichhorn and Schultens,
Gesenius did not reach a definite view on the remaining
words cited here, but made mention of the different meanings that had ben proposed.

Gesenius objects to meanings that had been given to words
in certain passages only, contrary to their meanings elsewhere. He objected, for example, to the translation of אפוא
I say, by Ziegler and others, in Prov. 6, 3, according to the
Arabic; but insists that it means only: *now, then.* Likewise:
ארמנות means only *palaces,* not also: *boundaries,* in Mic. 5,
44 (Mich. Supple., 128). The niphal of: באש means: *to be
hated, to be in bad repute,* not also: *to be strong,* in 1 Sam.
13, 4 (Supple., 146).

Gesenius appealed to the Aramaic usage for some words
that had been explained from the Arabic. The following
may serve as illustrations. He translated: גלם *to fold;*
גלום *mantle;* דגר *to gather.* The latter Michaelis translated: *to flee,* according to the Arabic. (Supple., 394).

From the later Hebrew of the Talmud, Gesenius explained,
for example: דדה *to proceed slowly, solemnly;* מהמרות *pits;*
and קרקר - קיר *to pull down a wall.*

In this first edition Gesenius separated by Roman numerals many roots which were formerly treated as one, and
which he later joined himself after he saw some connection.
He tries to avoid a merely conjectural connection. Thus he
would not equate: לין *to stay over night,* and: לון *to mur-
mer;* מהרI *to hurry* and II: *to buy,* ישןI *to be old* and II:
to sleep.

The dialects were compared for analogous idioms and
developed meanings. Thus: בבת - עין means: *the apple of
the eye,* lit., the maniquin of the eye. The Aramaic has: אישון
The idiom should not be explained from the Arabic as:
the gate of the eye. The development of meanings: *to cleave
to, to pursue, to reach* is found in the roots: דבק - لحق
that of: *to be liberal, generous, noble* is found in the roots:
נקב - נדק. From the primary meaning: *to bore, to pierce*
is developed the meaning: *to determine.*

The Hebrew usage itself yielded modifications of meaning in certain words and phrases. Of these we note:
גרם *to cut off,* with: ל *to lay up for* is analogous to: אצל - ל

נֶרֶם הבדיל ל. means: *bone;* by a comparison with עֶצֶם we deduce that it means also: *the same, the very same.*

Whereas his predecessors were bent on showing the relation of the Hebrew to the Arabic and studying out primary meanings, Gesenius devoted more space and time to the development of meanings. For example, Gesenius gave the meanings of: אָהֵב in the following order: (1) *to love;* (2) *to rejoice over something.* He makes no comparison with the cognate languages, although he is carefuly to verify each meaning with some passages. Simonis, 1793, had the primary meaning: *dilexit, amavit,* and made no effort to show the development of the other meanings. However, he compared the Hebrew with the Arabic and Samaritan to show that the fundamental Hebrew meaning must be: *to pant after something.* Eichhorn cited many more passages than are necessary. Instead of being valuable to illustrate the development of meanings, they show the different grammatical forms, many of which are perfectly regular. Besides, Gesenius also explained the use of this verb with particles, which Eichhorn failed to do.

Although Gesenius often gave fewer citations than Eichhorn, his are the more unusual ones. Thus, for example, Gesenius explained that the grammatical form *jecherash* means only: *to be silent, to be dumb;* while: *jacharosh* means: *to work with metals, plow.*

In general, Gesenius differed from his predecessors in this that he revised each entire article. Instead of accumulating a mass of unnecessary and often wrong material, he carefully sifted everything that his predecessors had done, freely discarded, and freely retained what he thought was necessary.

The main defects in the First Edition were the discussion of the Hebrew together with the Aramaic of the Bible, instead of having two distinct sections, and the fact that the lexicographical material was not so clearly separated from the etymological material in the article, as should have been desired. But even with the retention of these defects, the lexicon is much easier to consult than its predecessors.

Prof. E. Robinson gave the following estimate of the first lexicon published by Gesenius:[8]

---

[8] *Bibliotheca Sacra,* 1843, 361 ff.

This work exhibited that extensive and profound research,
that command of materials and sagacity in the use of them
which have placed its author in the first rank of modern
philologists. Many of the views and results, however,
evolved in the ardour and freshness of youthful pursuit, did
not stand the test of the author's own riper judgment and
investigations; and in later years he was accustomed to
look upon this as juvenile work. Still it opened up a new
and wide field of Hebrew literature; removed from that
study its repulsive aspect; and rendered it accessible to all.
So great was the success of this work, that the author was
immediately applied to by the publisher to construct a
lexicon of the New Testament on like principles.

An epitome for students, based on this larger work, was
published in 1815.[9] This manual is about one-half as large
as the First Edition. Space was saved by omitting all the
longer disquisitions, whereby particular significations had
been defended or opposed. This may be seen by comparing
the article on: אשרה in both lexicons. Passages that had
been quoted in full to exemplify various significations of
words and phrases were diminished probably by one-half
their number. In many cases the smaller work suffered
considerably by these omissions. References made to the
dialects, old versions, and exegetical books for a better elucidation of forms or meanings of words are much abbreviated
and often omitted altogether. The latter was especially the
case when the material was of such a nature that it might
not be available to the students. Everything was thus condensed as much as possible in order to make this a handy
students' edition. The first edition was to be reissued as a
thesaurus, which would take up matters more in detail.

But the Epitome is not a mere abstract of the preceding
edition. In it Gesenius introduced certain improvements
that he had made, especially in the materials of lexicography.

Thus some of the articles were shortened naturally because Gesenius had something more definite to substitute
for a long discussion. This was, for example, the case in
the article: איתן No. 3, where he now gave the meaning:
hard, disastrous (Luther: *bringt Wehe*), in Prov. 13, 15;
and: "The struggle in his limbs is terrible," in Job, 33, 19.
These quotations are missing in the preceding edition. Some
improvements were made in the articles: המן and פרע

---

[9] *Hebraeisch-deutsches Handlexicon*, 1815.

I. In Ezek. 5, 7, the form: המנכם is derived from the root: המן and translated: *because ye rage,* etc., instead of: *because ye have sinned,* as before. Changes in citations and meanings were made in the articles: און - אָון - אדם - אב. The article אָב is practically doubled. The figurative use: *priest, teacher,* is more thoroughly explained, and the meanings: *begetter* and *counselor* are added. A new article: אָב *wish* is inserted with its citation Job 34, 36. Many of the missing Ketib forms were supplied in this edition, but the attempt to mention all the Samaritan variants is discontinued.

In this edition Gesenius began to combine many roots that he had separated in the preceding edition, and distinguished by Roman numerals. The following are some of these roots: הדר had been treated as two roots in the 1810 Edition: I. *to honor;* II. *to swell.* Now both of these meanings are derived from the general meaning: *to be wide.* חלל whose meanings: I. *to pierce;* II. *to loose,* had been assigned to two different roots, is now considered one root, with the general meaning: *to pierce,* in spite of the fact that the Arab distinguished between two roots by means of a harder and a softer initial consonant. We note that Buhl, 16. Edition, has separated these roots again. In the edition of 1810, Gesenius had separated the meanings of: חבר under two roots: I. *to bind;* II. *to practice sorcery.* Now he joined them under the one root: *to bind,* and developed the second meaning by referring to the magic knot. The meanings: *to seek* and: *to dissemble,* of the root: חפש are brought together by means of the intermediate notion: *to allow oneself to be sought, to hide.* Thus we see Gesenius join some roots that his predecessors had already considered related; however, he does it, not by taking over a primary meaning from the Arabic, but rather by considering an inner relationship in the roots themselves.

In this edition, Gesenius also established some better etymological connections. Thus משעול *cavernous way* is now brought into connection with: שעל *hollow hand;* נחלל *passage for cattle,* with the root: נחל *to drive cattle.* עד *until, eternity* and: עדי *age* are now derived from: עדה *to pass away.*

On the other hand some roots that were formerly considered related were now separated. For example: חול

to turn and: יחל *to wait* had both been considered under: חול *to turn.* They were now divided; and so was: סכך I. *to cover;* II. *to plait.*

Many articles were revised by having their meanings put into a better order. Some of these are: נחם - נגד - כן - רוח - ראש.

The terminology of the lexicon was brought into conformity with that of the grammar. In regard to substantives, it is now indicated whether they are primitive, from a verb (verbal), or denominative (from a noun). In the latter case the word is referred to a substantive, e. g., לויתן is referred to the substantive: לויה *wreathe,* and it means: *coiled animal.* This, in turn, is derived from: לוה.

With respect to adverbs, prepositions, and conjunctions, it was indicated whether they were originally substantives or not; and the transition from adverb to preposition and conjunction was shown where it occurs. As regards these the construction with the preterite or the future is indicated. Cf. the articles: עד and תחת.

Improvements were also made in the study of gender, but here much remained to be done. Since the manual was intended for students, a very helpful index of difficult forms was added at the end.

The next edition of the German manual appeared in 1823.[10] It contains about the same amount of material as the previous edition. New in this edition are: the essay on the sources of Hebrew Philology and Lexicography, which we discussed in our first chapter, and a German vocabulary with page-references to the respective Hebrew words in the lexicon proper. The following improvements were attempted in this edition:

1. An attempt was made to put the roots which occur only in derivatives into their proper alphabetical order. Now a better connection between different words derived from the same root was established. Some roots which were revised and put into a better order were: אוה - אצל - און - אול (אולם). With respect to these roots, it should be noted also that Gesenius changed their primary meanings as he learned more about the root and its derivatives. Thus the

---

[10] *Hebraeisches und chaldaeisches Handwoerterbuch,* Zweite Auflage, 1823.

difficult root: אול in 1815, received the primary meaning:
to be strong; in 1823, *to be first,* according to the Arabic
comparison; in 1834, *to turn,* according to the analogy in
the Hebrew.

2. As in the preceding edition, Gesenius attempted to
establish the connection between more roots, which he had
separated, after a careful consideration of the relation of
ideas in the Hebrew. Gesenius contended that the Hebrew
usage had suffered at the hands of the later Dutch and their
followers in Germany, who on the basis of absurd etymologies had given many wrong primary meanings to Hebrew
words. At the same time, Gesenius admitted that he had
carefully studied the works of Albert Schultens, e. g., *Job*
and *Proverbs,* and those of N. W. Schroeder,[11] and obtained
much help from them.

3. In this edition, Gesenius also began to revise the
articles on the particles, especially: ב and ו and אם. His
desire was to arrange the meanings according to their Hebrew development, and not according to the German equivalents. However, he does not always begin with one primary
meaning. To: ב he gave three primary meanings: *in, at,
with,* following the old grammarians, and he forced all the
Hebrew meanings into this artificial scheme, instead of
beginning with the true primary meaning: *in.*

4. The comparisons with the cognate languages were revised and increased. Arabic and Syriac, the former of
which was used most extensively for the comparisons, were
printed in their own characters, while the Samaritan and
Ethiopic were given in Hebrew transcription. Definite
traces of an increased influence of the dialects may be
noted. Whereas Gesenius formerly was adverse to the taking of primary meanings from the dialects, he now introduced them more freely, where he thought them necessary.
This may be noted, for example, in the article: אול where
the Arabic: *to be first* was in this edition substituted for:
to be strong, as the primary meaning.

The publication of the second edition of his Manual Lexicon, which we have just discussed, marked an epoch in
Gesenius' grammatical and lexicographical labors. As early
as 1813, he had begun his grammatical labors by publishing

---

[11] *Geschichte der hebr. Sprache u. Schrift,* 129.

the first edition of his small grammar. His *Geschichte der
hebraeischen Sprache und Schrift* had been published in
1815, and his *Lehrgebaeude der hebraeischen Sprache*, in
1817. His learned commentary on Isaiah had been published in 1820-21. During the period of time intervening
between the publication of the first lexicon and the second
edition of the Manual, in 1823, Gesenius' labors had touched
upon all the chief branches of Hebrew philology, grammar,
lexicography, and interpretation; and his efforts had been
recognized the world over as those of a master mind.[12]
The next years were devoted to a recasting and republishing
of his former works, the collection and arrangement of materials for his Hebrew-Latin Thesaurus, and the preparation of
the third edition of his Manual Lexicon.

The third edition of the German Manual Lexicon was
published in 1828.[13] This edition shows an increase of 98
pages of lexicographical material over the preceding one.
But actually more was added, because a new and better
method of abbreviation had been introduced. The essay
on the sources of lexicography was also revised and aug-
mented. The following are some of the improvements that
Gesenius attempted in this edition:

1. Particular attention was paid to the etymological material. Once more Gesenius wished to supply all the roots
of words which are only derivations, even if these be proper-
nouns. These were discussed, in many instances, in connection with their roots; and through a study of the derivation, Gesenius tried to arrive at the correct primary meaning of the root. Let us note, for instance, the study of the
root: בּכר in connection with the derivative: בּכר *young
camel*. By giving the root: בּכר, according to the Arabic
comparison, the primary meaning: *to be early*, instead of:
to do early, as in the preceding edition, Gesenius arrived
at an inner connection between the two. The stress in the
derivative should therefore fall on the age, not on the spe-
cies. Similar changes were made in the articles: דרר - דבר
קצף - קוה The latter received the primary meaning: *to tear*,
from which: קצף *splinter* was developed.

As we noted, Gesenius in his First Edition, had been very

12 Robinson, *Bibliotheca Sacra*, 1843, 385.
13 *Hebraeisches und chaldaeisches Handwoerterbuch*, 1828.

cautious not to join homonymic roots that seemed to have no connection. Rather than make the mistake of his Dutch predecessors, who forced the roots together, he preferred to separate them by Roman numerals. In the 1815 and 1823 editions he had begun to recognize many of these connections. In the course of time, he established so many more relationships that the Roman numerals of the First Edition were diminished approximately by two-thirds. We may note a few more instances in which Gesenius' method of combining roots is shown. To the root: נדר he gave in this edition, the primary meaning: *to press* (*draengen*). Formerly he recognized a: נדר II, with the primary meaning: *to cut in.* He now made the connection between the two by comparing them with the Arabic: جدر which he translated: *to cut grape-vines,* and this is properly, he said: *to press in with a knife.* In like manner, he established a relation between the meanings: *to cut* and *to crowd together* (*sich zusammendraengen*). Other roots which he treated in one article were: חמם - חרש - זמר - גור. There are many more between which he surmised that a connection existed, but he did not yet attempt to make it.

Once more, Gesenius repeated that the fact that a Hebrew root appears in the Arabic in two forms, with a harder and a softer pronunciation, does not show that two roots must necessarily have existed in the Hebrew. It may be that the Hebrew roots developed another meaning which was never distinguished by another pronunciation, whereas the Arabic made the distinction. He therefore treated as one root: בצע which appears in the Arabic as بضع and بصع. The Hebrew means: *to cut,* from which: *to make gain* is developed. In like manner he treated: חלל *to pierce* and *to loosen,* which appears in the Arabic as: خل *to pierce,* and حل *to loosen.* On the other hand, Gesenius took notice of the fact that all the meanings of a root were not necessarily derived from one primary meaning. Many meanings slipped in accidentally. Gesenius detected such a borrowed meaning in the root: נאל which means *to demand back.* The meaning: *to be polluted* is not a development of this meaning, but is borrowed from the root: געל. The root נאל is therefore to be treated as two articles.

In the determination of primary meanings Gesenius now

paid more attention to the fundamental notions lying at the
base of a group of roots. This primary notion is found, for
example, in a group of roots with the strong consonants:
פם - רע - פיץ which always express the idea of *splitting* when
they are lengthened to three-radical words.

2. In the Third Edition, Gesenius also made considerable
change in the articles on the particles. He was now thoroughly convinced that all the particles, even those that con-
sist of only one letter, are mutilated forms of complete
words, very likely nominal forms. This necessitated a further study of their etymology.

3. An attempt was made to include all the proper-nouns
which had been omitted in former editions, for example,
those that occurred but once or were of little value for the
elucidation of roots. Now, proper-nouns of no special historical interest were mentioned, with the citations where
they occur.

4. Gesenius claimed that he went over the lexicon in
detail very carefully and corrected the mistakes. He acknowledged his indebtedness to several men who had contributed corrections.

Johann Ulrich Faesi wrote a very thorough and extensive
review of this edition,[14] in connection with his review of
the new edition of Simonis' Lexicon, edited by Winer.[15]
In this review, Faesi discussed in how far Gesenius had been
able to live up to the principles which he had set out to
follow. Space permits me to mention only a few details of
the long review.

Faesi showed that Gesenius neglected many of the verbal
forms that deviated from the regular paradigm, that he did
not give all of the constructions and phrases, nor all the
variants of the ketib and the keri. Examples are produced
in great number as evidence.[16]

Faesi also found many instances in which Gesenius did
not approach the correct fundamental meaning of the root.
For example, Gesenius derived: חב from the root: חבב
thus making a concrete notion depend on what is purely an
abstract idea, whereas: חבב is more likely a denominative
of: חב . As regards: חכה Gesenius entertained the curious

---

[14] *Neue Jahrbuecher fuer Philologie u. Paedagogik*, IV, 1832, 155 ff.
[15] *Joh. Simonis Lexicon Manuale*, Ed. G. B. Winer, 1828.
[16] Faesi, *loc. cit.*, 156 f.

notion that it is a feminine of: חֵך *gum,* and means *hook* because the hook catches in the gum of a fish. Gesenius also often passed by fine distinctions in synonyms. For instance, he classified the roots: חלף and עבר as identical in meaning, whereas there is a distinct shade of difference: one means: *to go over,* the other: *to glide over.*

The reviewer also objected to the derivation of all the particles from nouns. For example, Gesenius derived ב from בית [17]; כן from הכן ; ל from עַל - אֶל ; and כ from כן; Gesenius based his contention on the theory that the particles had developed later in the language than the substantives and verbs.[18]

Faesi showed that the arrangement of the meanings, especially of the particles, is still very faulty. For instance, the article ב still has all its meanings arranged according to the three fundamental meanings: *in, at,* and *with.* Faesi objected, for insufficient reasons, to the placing of the phrase: שתה - ב under: *in,* because Faesi looked upon this ב as a ב of means: *to drink by means of.* He noted that the arrangement of meanings in the article: עֵד is faulty. Gesenius had only three divisions: A. substantive; B. preposition; C. conjunction. He omitted the adverbial use altogether. The arrangement of the meanings in the article: כי rested on the wrong notion that it was originally a relative like אשר and not a demonstrative.

Gesenius succeeded in taking in most of the proper-nouns, but he failed in the correction of detail. The work, as Faesi shows,[19] abounded in all kinds of mistakes in citations, quotations, and references. Faesi rightly suggested that a lexicon which had won for itself the envious distinction of almost exclusive authority should be a little more exact in the details. This work was really too much for one man, and Gesenius should have had colaborators.[20] Faesi's contention on all these points was well-founded.

Of the three editions of the Manual Lexicon, just compared, each was published in three thousand copies, which were sold out very rapidly.[21]

At this period of time a noteworthy change occurred in

---

[17] Not removed till the 10. Ed.
[18] Faesi, *op. cit.,* 177.
[19] Faesi, *loc. cit.,* 205 ff.
[20] *Ibidem,* 206.
[21] *Bibliotheca Sacra,* 1843, 364.

Gesenius' lexicographical labors. So far Gesenius had been
the leader of the great movement to advance the study of
Hebrew. His works were considered authoritative. But
now others arose who penetrated ever deeper than he into
the mysteries of the language. De Sacy and his pupils had
done much to put the best Arabic literature before scholars;
Bopp and Grimm had made an impression on the scholars
with their comparative studies in the Indo-European languages. Hebrew was also influenced by the Indo-European
studies. Hupfeld and Ewald anticipated Gesenius in using
these new sources for the study of Hebrew lexicography.
The latter's grammar, published in 1827, was hailed with
delight by many because of its philosophic studies in the
history of words.

This new movement did not influence the nature of the
first *fasciculus* of Gesenius' Thesaurus, published in 1829,
but the Latin edition of the Manual Lexicon, already in
preparation in 1827, was influenced by it, so that it did not
appear till 1833. This new movement, also changing Gesenius' views considerably, called forth from him the motto:
Dies diem docet, which now first appears on the fly-leaf
of the Latin Manual; and has been on the fly-leaf of all his
manual lexicons since.

The Latin Manual[22] was prepared at the request of many
foreign students, in England, Holland, and America. Gesenius had intended that this should be little more than a
translation of his German manual lexicon, of 1828,[23] but as
we saw before, he had to take note of the recent philological
investigations. The publication of the Thesaurus was inter-
rupted; so that he could devote all his time to these new
investigations.

The Latin Manual is therefore a new work. The articles
on the first three letters of the alphabeth were corrected
in accordance with the material in the Thesaurus. The remainder was not a translation of the German edition, but
much was added.

1. A more thorough investigation was made of the internal and native force of the Hebrew roots, begun in the
Third Edition. Once more Gesenius made the statement that

22 Gesenius, *Lexicon Manualis,* 1833, ix.
23 *Bibliotheca Sacra,* 1843, 366.

the Hebrew usage oftener determines the usage of the related dialects than *vice versa*.[24] The connection between the different elements of Hebrew roots was more closely observed. Gesenius found that three-radical roots can often be traced to two-radical roots, most of which are onomatopoetical. Thus it was possible to trace words of quite diverse signification to a single primary notion. Gesenius considered the ascertainment of the primary sense one of the most difficult tasks of the lexicographer, because of the fact that the intermediate stages of the developments have often been lost.

2. New in this edition were the comparisons with the Indo-European languages. Gesenius did not think that the relationship between the two language-groups was so close as had been supposed. We may note some of Gesenius' comparisons. The word: נער is compared with the Sanskrit: *nari* and *nara,* the Greek: ἀνήρ the Zend: *naere,* the Persian نار . אחר is compared with the Sansk. *eka* and the Pahlavi: *advek.* Gesenius made a study of the roots: פ - מל - בל and said that they all contain the primary meaning: *to fall.* They are compared with the Greek: σφάλλω the Latin, *fallo,* the German, *fallen,* and the English, *to fail.* Hebrew developments of this primary notion are: אבל - נבל - אפל - אמל. The latter refers to loosely hanging and withering leaves. The same notion is found in the Sanskrit: *pala,* straw, and *bali,* wrinkle. The root חקה received the primary meaning: *to hack.* This primary notion is found in the German: *hacken, hauen,* and in the Arabic: هلك

هق. All the words that have: חק as the primary syllable are considered onomatopoetic. אבק to strike is compared with the German: *pochen,* and is related to the syllables: רך - דק - פק - פנ - בך.

In these comparisons, it is to be noted that Gesenius was concerned mainly with linguistical analogies. He did not make the minute study of comparing syllable with syllable, which Fuerst made later on in his lexicon.[25] Fuerst followed very closely: Bopp, *Vergleichende Grammatik;* Pott, *Etymologische Forschungen;* and Rosen, *Radices sanscritae.*

---

[24] Gesenius, *Lexicon Manualis,* 1833, vii: *quarum loquendi usus saepius ex hebraeo utpote antiquiore pendere videtur, quam contra.*
[25] Fuerst, *Hebraeisches und Chaldaeisches Handwoerterbuch,* 1857-1861; 2 Ed. 1863 and 1876 Ed. 3, by Ryssel. This was also translated into English.

He used this still unverified material so extravagantly that
the theory lost most of its plausibility in spite of the fundamental possible reality at the basis of it.[26]

3. As before, Gesenius used the other dialects mainly for
the etymology and the explanation of forms. The word:
חֲזִיר for example, he compared with the Arabic: خِنْزِير . This
word has an inserted *nun,* and means: *swine,* from the verb:
خَزَر *to have small eyes.*

4. In this edition Gesenius exercised greater care with
regard to the arrangement of meanings. He acknowledged his indebtedness to Winer, whose edition of Simonis'
Lexicon had surpassed his work in this respect.

5. The articles on the particles and pronouns were also
revised. For these Gesenius made use of the material which
Winer had contributed to the study of Hebrew usage, but he
objected to much that had been obtained from the Latin
and Greek as being too artificial and forced.

The Latin Manual contained the grammatical analytical index, as well as the Latin index, but the essay on the sources
of Hebrew lexicography was omitted.

The German Manual based on this Latin edition was published in 1834.[27] It contains many of the corrections and
additions which are contained in the Latin Manual. These
corrections are more extensive in the first half of the lexicon
than in the second, since the second half was printed as
early as 1832. The first part, embracing the letters: א to מ
appeared later, and a more thorough use could be made
of Faesi's review of the previous edition.

The relation between the Fourth Edition and the Third
German Edition is the following:

1. As in the previous Latin edition, the study of the
etymology was advanced. This improvement was made not
so much on the basis of a comparison with the cognate languages as of the study of the sounds in the Hebrew language
itself. More Hebrew roots are traced to one-syllable roots,
many of which are onomatopoetic. It may be well to add a
few more illustrations beyond those that we discussed in

---

[26] Cf. Apendix in Ryssel-Fuerst, *Hebraeisches und Chaldaeisches
handwoerterbuch,* 1876.
[27] Gesenius, *Hebraeisches und Chaldaeisches Handwoerterbuch ueber
das Alte Testament,* 1834. Vierte Ausgabe.

connection with the Latin Manual, to show Gesenius' method.
In Ges. Ed. 3. the meanings of: אהב were arranged as follows: (1) *to love;* (2) *to rejoice over something, wish for.*
The first use was compared with the Greek: ἀγαπάω and
the second, with the use of: ἀγαπάω in 2 Tim. 4, 8: *those
who desire his appearance,* and with the Arabic: حب

and وَدَّ . In the Latin Manual and the German edition,
of 1834, the meanings had been arranged: (1) *to desire;*
(2) *to love;* (3) with ל *to do something gladly,* as: *aimer à
faire quelque chose.* The primary meaning was changed to:
aspiravit ad aliquid, which is related to the primary meanings in: או-אב-הב cf. חבב-אבל חב - אבה-אוה-חות.
כפן was listed in Ges. Ed. 3. as a root that does not occur,
but whose counterpart is the Samaritan: כפן which means:
to be athirst, used in Ezek. 17, 7, of the roots of a grape-vine.
In Ges. Ed. 4. the word is referred to the root: גבן *to be
crooked,* Arab., جفن *eye-brow.* The primary meaning is
therefore: *to be crooked.* He also called attention to the
relation existing between words whose middle consonant
has been softened to: ו or י. He showed that there is a
connection between: ריח and רוח-חבל and חול.

The ascertainment of a primary meaning underlying a
group of roots led to the diminution of the number of roots
that had formerly been separated by Roman numerals. It is
interesting to note how Gesenius established some of these
connections. In Ges. Ed. 3., two roots were recognized for:
אהל one with the meaning: *to glitter,* the other, *to break
camp.* In Ges. Ed. of 1815, he had had only one root, and
inclined toward the derivation *to glitter, shine,* in the passage Job 25, 5, by saying: *the moon does not dwell there.*
In Ges. Ed. 4. the meaning: *to shine,* from this root, as well
as the roots: הלל and هل is considered the derived
meaning of: *to break up camp* (lit., *to tent, zelten*), by
bringing in the idea that the tent glitters in the distance.
On p. xliv, Gesenius mentioned 24 roots that he combined
in a similar manner, in this edition.

Gesenius repeated his warning that all homonymic roots
need not necessarily have the same primary meaning.
Neither is the objection justified that two Hebrew roots are
unrelated because they appear in the Arabic in different

pronunciations. These roots may accidentally have received a different orthography through carelessness in ordinary use.

2. The Indo-Germanic also found a place in this edition. The comparisons which Gesenius included here are not so numerous as those in the Latin Manual. He believed in an historic relationship between the two language-groups, but he did not undertake a thorough treatment of it. He contented himself here, as in the Latin Manual, with certain interesting analogies. In the case of: ל though, we find that the Indo-Germanic influenced him to give to the Hebrew what it is not known to possess, namely, a diminutive: ל Gesenius said that it is often added to three-radical words to make a diminutive of them. As examples he cited: כרם *orchard;* כרמל *a small garden;* גבע *calyx;* גבעל *small calyx.* Gesenius based this solely on the analogies found in Greek, Latin, and German. This diminutive element was discarded soon after for lack of evidence.

Although these comparisons were interesting, they consumed too much space, as may be seen, for instance, by consulting the article: נדד. Gesenius compared this verb with a series of roots whose primary meaning is: *to surround, fence-in.* This was compared with those Indo-European words which have the underlying notion: *to enclose.* As such he mentioned the Middle Latin: *cadarum;* the Italian: *catarata;* the German: *Gatter, Gitter.* He found a transposition in the words: χόρτος *hortus, cors, Garten, Gard,* e. g., in *Stuttgard;* Slav., *gorod,* etc.

3. The articles on the particles were improved considerably over the preceding edition, those of the first letters of the alphabet especially, e. g. כן - כ - זה - הוא - בעד - ב - מה - מי - כי - על He made use of the new material that had been contributed to the study of particles by Winer. At the same time he did not give up his own views in every case. He, for example, still maintained that: ב is derived from בי or בית. Instead of giving it three primary meanings, he now recognized *in* to be the primary meaning. He did not accept Faesi's criticism of the phrase: שתה - ב as a ב of means: *to drink by means of;* but he retained that it refers to a drinking of the contents of a vessel, and referred to the analogy in the Indo Germanic languages. Gesenius also retained the idea that the three prefixed particles are not

original forms, but abbreviations. He considered, for example, אַן to be an original substantive, likewise many of the other particles. There is a decided improvement in the primary meanings as well as in the logical arrangement of the meanings in the articles on the particles.

In this brief review of Gesenius' lexicons, it was, naturally quite impossible to show fully how great were the improvements which were made from one edition to another. He made a serious attempt to interpret the language of the Old Testament, as it was handed down to us, and in this he achieved noteworthy success. In the interpretation of the inner relationship existing between the different manifestations of the Hebrew language, its usage and its etymology, he went far beyond what his predecessors had done. But it has been rightly said that neither Gesenius, nor his predecessor Michaelis, showed the philosophic ability in the study of the inner relationships which Dietrich displayed later.

The main weakness in Gesenius' work, notably in the last edition of his manual, was his failure to divide the Hebrew roots according to sister languages. It seems as though all homonymic roots looked related to him, and he made desperate efforts to bring them together. The result was that he gave some roots very uncertain primary meanings, and from them made some unlikely developments. Many roots were combined, which, as far as any one can see, cannot be brought together on the basis of the knowledge that we possess. For instance זָלַל had been correctly divided in Ges. Ed. of 1815, into the two roots: I. *to be despised;* II. Niph. *to be shaken.* In Ges. Ed. 4. the two roots were joined. In order to join them, Gesenius began with three primary meanings: *to tremble, to shake, to pour.* From these he developed: (1) *to shake;* (2) *to pour out.* However, the Arabic has two roots: زَلَّ *to slip,* and ذَلَّ *to be low, to be despised,* and therefore a separation into two roots is justified. The same may be said of the article: אָהַל in which Gesenius attempted to derive the meaning: *to shine* from: *to tent,* in a very unlikely manner.

On the other hand, but in rarer instances, Gesenius split roots that belonged together. For example, he could not see how the word: פֶּלֶג *canal* could be derived from the root: פָּלַג : *to divide;* so he had to supply another root, with the

meaning: *to wave, to roll*. But *canal* is very easily derived
by saying that it is something that divides the land.

Some of Gesenius' primary meanings were not the result
of a careful comparison of the Hebrew, but were taken over
directly from the cognate tongues. Thus he gave to: שָׁקַר
to lie, the primary meaning: *to color the truth* because the

Arabic has: شَقَّ   *to be red*. In the same manner, פָּדַר the
root for: פָּדַר *fat*, received the primary meaning: *to feed*,
for the sake of the Arabic: فَدَّنَ *to feed cattle*. A hasty
consideration of some of these fundamental meanings might
induce one to suppose that Gesenius ended by doing just that
which he had criticized most severely in his predecessors,
that is, that he simply took over an Arabic meaning and
tried to develop the Hebrew meaning from it. Closer in-
spection reveals that these are only isolated instances. Some
of his primary meanings are, of course, little more than
guesses, but many of them are the result of a very careful
comparison of the Hebrew relationships, while the cognate
tongues are called upon for confirmation.

A wrong primary meaning quite naturally dislocated the
correct order of the developed meanings. This we saw
happened in the case of the root: אָהֵב to which Gesenius
gave the primary meaning: *aspiravit ad aliquid,* with the
result that the natural order of meanings: (1) *to love;* (2)
to desire, had to give way to the reverse: (1) *to desire;*
(2) *to love.*

In his use of the cognate dialects Gesenius compared the
Arabic and the Aramaic most of all, they being of greatest
importance for Hebrew lexicography. But his Thesaurus
especially, reveals that he had a very extensive knowledge
of all of the other cognate languages also. He made great
advances in the use of the Rabbinical literature, as time
went on. Since the cuneiform literature was not available
at Gesenius' time, he had to forego the rich treasures which
it presents. He often gave only the Greek equivalents to
Assyrian proper-nouns, and tried to explain their etymology
from the Persian. It is interesting to note one etymology of
an Assyrian proper-noun, which Gesenius rendered with
surprising correctness. He surmised that Evil Merodach
אֱוִיל-מְרֹדַךְ was originally an Assyrian or Persian name, which
meant: *a worshipper of Merodach;* however, he believed

that the Hebrew conveyed the idea of foolishness in the word: אֱוִיל, which is impossible.

That Gesenius progressed considerably in his etymologies may be seen from the fact that he diminished the number of substantives which he had considered primary to less than half of the original number. Nouns, as: אָב and: אֵם he considered primary nouns, emanating from the nursery. In his Thesaurus and in his grammatical treatment, he was forced, for the sake of convenience, to refer them to their supposed roots.

Gesenius' strong point was his ability to investigate impartially. He made not only original contributions, but he had the persistence and the ability to reconsider the work done by others. He made rigorous corrections and revisions in his own work, as well as in the work of others. In his last edition he improved the articles on the particles and prepositions where Winer, ed. Simonis (1828), had showed him the way. In the grammar, beginning with the tenth edition, he applied the results of Hupfeld's work, especially in phonetics. And he also derived benefit from the work of Ewald. Of all this he made discriminate use. He was, as may be said in general, a man of no pet theories, willing to change his views, when he was convinced that he was in error, as may be noted in the Thesaurus. Very often he explained the same matter in different ways in different parts of the book. Gesenius showed the qualities necessary for a skilled lexicographer in this that he kept a sane, level balance, and usually adopted only that which was good and applicable.

The value of the materials in Gesenius' lexicons was greatly enhanced by their presentation. Gesenius understood how to present his own materials as well as those of others, in a clearer and more harmonic fashion than had been done before. His explanations have the sincerity and ease which commend themselves to students. Although Faesi conceded that the materials of Winer's edition of Simonis, Lexicon were, as a whole, better than those of Ges. Ed. 3., he nevertheless preferred the latter as embodying a clearness of presentation and comprehensibility of style that was unsurpassed.[28]

---

[28] Faesi, *op. cit.*, 236 f.

The fact that Gesenius' Lexicon was in German instead of
in Latin, and according to the alphabetic arrangement of
words must not be underestimated in studying what contributed to its unbounded popularity. This, together with
a judicious use of the work of others, as well as his own,
and an attractive presentation enabled Gesenius to attain
and to hold the foremost place in modern Hebrew lexicography.

CHAPTER III

Twenty-three years after the untimely death of Gesenius, the Manual Lexicon was re-edited by Franz Eduard Christoph Dietrich (1810-1883). Dietrich was a man of extensive philological training. He had spent the years 1829-33 at the universities of Leipzig and Halle, where he was primarily a student of theology and Oriental subjects. At Halle, he must have come into contact with Gesenius, although I have no evidence to show that he actually did. Later he was instructor in the Semitic and European languages, in the University of Marburg. He lectured on Gothic, Nordic, Old Saxon, Anglo Saxon, German grammar, and versification, Old High German, Middle High German, and New High German history of literature. In the sixties, he gave up his lectures on Germanics to devote himself exclusively to Oriental subjects.[1] That Dietrich was successful in his Semitic studies is vouched for by McCurdy, who called him "the most thorough Semitic etymologist of the last generation."[2]

Dietrich was an ardent follower of Gesenius in this that he considered it to be of prime importance to study Hebrew from its own life and manifestations, before consulting the related tongues or the Indo-Germanic languages. We noticed that Gesenius did not make such an intense study of the relation existing between the Indo-Germanic and Semitic languages, as, for instance, Fuerst had attempted to do. He contented himself mainly with some comparisons, based on a similarity of sounds. Others had gone much further than Gesenius, and Dietrich registered strong objections to the injustice that Hebrew was receiving at the hands of those

---

[1] *Allgemeine Deutsche Biographie*, LX, 733.
[2] *American Journal of Philology*, 1883, 343.

who applied the Indo-Germanic languages wrongly. Dietrich says:[3]

One of the main reasons for the identification of Semitic
languages with the Indo-Germanic and for the intermingling
of similar shadings of sound may be sought in the false
premise that each one of the principle sounds of a language
possesses an inherent fundamental notion. If this were
actually the case, it would make little difference which people made use of this sound and how they articulated it.
However apparent the categories may seem to be which
Plato exhibited in Cratylus, where he attributed to certain
Greek sounds perceptions of their own,—the entire hypothesis is a phantastical product, of which Plato exhibited
many in a half-sincere, half-jesting manner. Recent discoveries in the history of language have taught us that the oldest,
simplest roots in a language are syllables, not letters of the
alphabeth. When the sounds are combined, we first have
the picture of a perception, a sound in nature, or a thought.
Not the separate element, but the higher union of a living
combination of sounds has a concrete meaning embodied
in it. The assertion that the sense of words is found in
these syllables, and not in the sounds as such, has gratuit-
ously come to light in these studies.

Dietrich says that the etymology of words should be obtained by studying the synonymns of the Hebrew itself, as
well as those of the related tongues. When these have been
classified the underlying psychological factor can often be
determined.

Dietrich published only three editions of the lexicon, and
of these the difference between the Sixth and the Seventh
Edition is very slight. The relation between the Fifth Edition[4] and the Fourth is the following:

[3] *Abhandlungen fuer semitische Wortforschung*, 1844, vii: Ein haupt-
saechlicher Grund jener Identificirung des Semitischen mit dem Indo-
germanischen und dieser Vermischung verwandter Lautfaerbungen mag
der Satz sein, dass jedem der Hauptsprachlaute fuer sich eine be-
stimmte Grundanschauung zukomme, in welchem Falle es allerdings zur
Sache wenig taete, welches Volk diesen Laut ausgesprochen hat, und
mit welchem Grade von Artikulation und Haerte. Aber wie scheinbar
auch die Kategorieen sind, die Plato im Cratylus einzelnen griechischen
Lauten beigelegt hat, die ganze Hypothese ist eins der Phantasiegebilde,
deren uns Plato so manche halb ernst, halb neckend ausgesponnen hat.
Die nun zugaenglicher gewordene Sprachgeschichte hat gelehrt, dass
auch die aeltesten einfachsten Sprachwurzeln Sylben, nicht Buchstaben
sind. Ihnen, den Lauten in ihrer Einigung kommt erst zu, das Bild
einer Anschauung, eines Naturlautes oder eines Gedankens zu sein, nicht
das einzelne Element, sondern die hoehere Einheit einer lebendigen
Lautverbindung bedeutet etwas Konkretes. Die Behauptung, dass in
diesen Sylben nicht in den Einzelnen als solchen der Wortsinn liege,
hat sich ungesucht in den ersten der vorliegenden Abhandlungen ergeben.
[4] Dietrich, F. D. C., *Hebraeisches und chaldaeisches Handwoerterbuch*.
Von Wilhelm Gesenius, 1857.

In the Fifth Edition, Dietrich decided to make no changes in explanations and declarations which in any way depended upon Gesenius' dogmatic concepts. The articles עבד - יהוה and עמנואל were therefore left unaltered. In exegetical matters he allowed himself to introduce only such improvements as are found in the latter parts of the Thesaurus. Dietrich took practically nothing from the numerous commentaries which had appeared after the death of Gesenius. He wished to preserve the literary character in the book as it had been left by Gesenius.

Dietrich made a thorough revision of the etymology, the meanings, and the comparisons with kindred dialects. In order that Gesenius should not be held responsible for the additions, Dietrich had inserted this new material in brackets, but he did not indicate where he had cancelled material. Changes were made in the study of the etymology of the pronouns and particles. According to Hupfeld and Ewald, pronominal forms were to be derived from original pronominal roots, and not from verbal and nominal roots.[5] Dietrich dropped, for, example, the root: הלא removal for: הלאה likewise the root: אדה for אדין and הלם for הלום: Gesenius himself had begun these changes in the notes for a new edition of his Latin Manual.[6]

Likewise Dietrich diminished the number of nouns that had been considered primitives still more. With the exception of a few abstract notions and some numerals, whose root was omitted to save space, all the nouns are now derived from verbal-roots. According to Dietrich, Gesenius 1810-13 had regarded most of the nouns, and without exception the one-syllable nouns, as primitives. These were diminished by half in 1833 and 1834; and these were again diminished in the sections of the Thesaurus belonging to the years 1840 and 1842. Likewise the number of nouns considered primitives were reduced from time to time in the editions of the grammar. In Part V. of the Thesaurus, seven words for members of the body, as: רגל - ראש - קרן were derived from verbal roots. In the last fasciculus of the Thesaurus, prepared by Roediger, there are no more primitives. Dietrich attempted to find etymologies for more of

---

[5] Hupfeld, *System der Demonstrativbildung*, in *Zt. f. Kunde des Morgenlandes*, II, 124 ff. 427.
[6] Published by A. Hoffmann in 1857.

the one-syllable nouns. He derived the noun: הר from the
Arabic هرّ horruit; עין from the roots: ענה - עון - עין
to bend, whence: eye, lit. a circle. He derived the trouble-
some: אָב from the root: אבב to bring forth, and אם from
אמם to precede, a root found only in the Arabic, as are most
of the roots which he introduced for one-syllable words.

The etymology of other words, not necessarily of one-
syllable, was altered because Dietrich objcted to the phonetic observations on which they were based. He objected
to the misuse of the theory that many sounds undergo a
softening of their original character. He derived: אשראל
from: אשר II instead of from אסר. For phonetic reasons
he also dropped the roots: גגג for: גג roof; בום for במה
and others. He dropped other roots because he considered
the softening of the נ to ן unlikely; for instance: דנץ and
חנח - דוץ and חוח . In the section of the Thesaurus published in 1840, Gesenius retracted the equation of: עור and
ענק - עפר and עוק which are found in the section published
in 1835; also the equation of: פנק and פוק found in Gesenius Ed. 4. In the latter sections of the Thesaurus, Gesenius
had attempted new equations, e. g., קוץ and קוא As regards
permutations, Dietrich made the general statement that similar or even like meaning does not justify the supposition
that a permutation has occurred. The relation of the younger
to the older period in the language must be considered. On
the wrong principle that like meaning signifies that a permutation has occurred, a permutation of almost any two
sounds could be made.

Dietrich also made changes in the determination of primary meanings. His principle was: whenever a concrete
primary notion cannot be ascertained from fixed verbal
meanings, nor from derivations belonging to an ancient state
of the language, in which this particular root still had a
different meaning, only the nearest Hebrew roots and the
cognate languages are to be the basis for the determination
of the original meaning; not non-Semitic roots, even if they
should have like sounds. Primary meanings based on a comparison of the Latin and Greek were eliminated, even where
it was difficult to find something more definite to replace
them, from the scattered traces of the Semitic stock. The
comparison with the Indo-European languages should not

begin before the primary meanings of the Semitic roots have been studied in their own Semitic relations. Dropped or determined otherwise were many primary meanings based solely on a similarity of sound. Gesenius, in Ed. 4. gave to: אבק the primary meaning: *to rap (pochen)*. Dietrich changed this to: *to coil, to wind,* whence: אבק *something that winds itself.* He gave to: כלף the primary meaning: *to grab, to lay hold of,* related to: כלב - כלא. Ges. in Ed. 4. gave the primary meaning: *to pound, (klopfen).* For: דמם Ges. in Ed. 4. gave the primary meaning: *to be dumb (stumm sein).* Dietrich changed this to: *to stroke,* from the Arabic: כֹּם In this way a considerable number of primary meanings were changed.

An attempt was made to trace roots to concrete primary meanings. Dietrich, for example, referred the noun: און to which Ges. Ed. 4. gave the abstract primary meaning: *non-existence (Nichtsein),* to the root: אנן *to breathe slowly.*

Words with the same radicals were treated as homonyms when it could be shown that they had originated in different ways. That certain homonymic roots are unrelated, although they have the same radicals, can be seen from the fact that the dialects distinguish them with a slight difference in pronunciation. On the basis of this, Dietrich distinguished נקש I: *to lay a snare,* which he equated with: יקש and קוש from נקק - נקף which are found in the Aramaic as: נקש *to thrust (stoszen).* One root: אפר was derived from the root: אף the other, from: פר In this manner Dietrich separated a number of roots which Gesenius had brought together.

The development of meanings in the Hebrew, Dietrich found hard to follow due to the varied character of the Hebrew word-development, resting as it does on the peculiar psychology of the Orient. Gesenius had contributed much to make the inner relation between different meanings comprehensible. On the basis of Hebrew analogies, careful comparisons with the dialects, and due attention to the permutations, he could show the relation existing between many seemingly unrelated meanings. Dietrich found this work, which Gesenius had begun, not nearly complete. It is done thoroughly only the last two letters of the alphabet in

the part of the Thesaurus issued by Roediger. In this edition, Dietrich included what Roediger had added under
these two letters. Some of the roots which Gesenius had
separated by Roman numerals were therefore joined after
studying the inner connection more thoroughly. Gesenius,
in Ed. 4., for example, had given two ארה roots namely:
I. *to pluck;* II. *to burn,* found in the Arabic. The word:
אריאל was developed from No. II. Dietrich gave one root
with the primary meaning: *to pierce (stechen),* cf. ארר
whence he derived the following meanings: 1. *ignite (anbren-
nen, (Feuer anstecken);* 2. *hollow-out, gouge (aushoehlen,
ausstechen).* In Ges. Ed. 4.: בדד was separated into:
I. *to separate oneself;* II. *to speak foolishly.* In Ges. Ed. 4.
פסח had been separated into: I. *to pass over;* II. *to limp,*
according to the Arabic. Dietrich gave one fundamental
meaning: *to cut,* and from this he developed: *to pass over.*
To limp was derived from the passive primary meaning:
*to be separated (aufgeloest sein), to be weak in one's mem-
bers.* In this way, Dietrich brought together many more
roots.

Dietrich listed the most difficult quadriliterals without
explanations. He did not care to adhere to what he considered an unfortunate theory, that these words are the combination of two triliteral roots. There were a few quinque-
literals which he considered combinations, e. g., those which
he says are clearly the combination of an absolute and a construct case. Thus he derived: צלמות from צל and מות
Other words that lack a clear derivation, such as סמדר and
חשמל he listed without an explanation.

The grammatical explanations of difficult verbal and nominal forms were given in harmony with Gesenius' grammar,
as revised by Roediger. Here and there one explanation was
substituted for the two former ones which had been in
doubt. As illustrations of what Dietrich did in this respect
we may note, for example, some changes that he made in
segolates ending in Waw. In Ges. Ed. 4. *ketsev* and *kâtsu* had
been listed as alternate forms. Dietrich recognized only *kâtsu*
to be the absolute form. Both: *derâôn* and *derâon* had been
considered absolute forms in Ges. Ed. 4. Dietrich recognized the latter to be the construct of the former. To: נאות
in Ges. Ed. 4, the root: נאה was given; Dietrich derived it
from: נוה. He made many other grammatical corrections.

The German appendix was revised by Dietrich himself. He supplied the references to some of the usual Hebrew expressions that had been omitted in the German. Dietrich spent three years in the preparation of the fifth edition of the lexicon.

The sixth edition of the Manual Lexicon was published by Dietrich, in 1863.

In this edition Dietrich followed the same principles as before. He endeavored to preserve Gesenius' literary character in the lexicon. Therefore he left the most important exegetical matters unchanged.[7] An attempt was made to use more thoroughly the material as it is found in the latter sections of the Thesaurus, notably that which had appeared subsequently to the article: Yad, and had been published after the fourth edition of the Manual.

More changes were made in etymology. We may consider a few of these here. In Ges. Ed. 4. אגרת had been derived from the root: אגר II according to the Persian, following Lorsbach; Dietrich surmised that there exists a relation to the Zend: hañkârayêmi, I announce. Ges. Ed. 4. had explained: חשמל as a composite noun from: נחש gold and: מל a root with the notion: to be smooth. Dietrich derived it from the root: חמש to glow, to glitter. Other words whose etymology was altered were: צאן - פוד - ספר - נחשת קשאים - צקלג, etc.

More changes were made in primary meanings. For example, ערל in Ges. Ed. 4. had received the primary meaning: to be uncircumcised; Dietrich 6. Ed. gave: to be rough, unclean, cf. פגע . ערם in Ges. 4. Ed. received the meaning: to be exhausted; Dietrich gave: to be soft, according to the Arabic comparison: فجر . To פקד Ges. 4. Ed. had given the primary meaning: to touch, to bump against, like: פגע and פגש. Dietrich said that the primary meaning is: to separate, like cerno, and this made it necessary for him to rearrange the developed meanings. Besides these, Dietrich changed the primary meanings of: רקם - רמש - צנן - ארה The primary meaning: das Ueber, for: עבר Dietrich rightly said is just based on sounds.

Dietrich also devoted some attention to the materials of the explanations, especially in archaeology. A number of

---

[7] He changed it in: עמנואל.

articles on weights and measures were revised. In regard
to proper-nouns, Dietrich attempted to supply those that
had been omitted, together with their explanations. New material was used in the location of geographical places. This
was the case not only for such well-known places as Sinai,
Rafidim, Shur, Bosra, and Kadesh, but also for lesser-known
cities, mountains, and wadis of Palestine. Dietrich took exception to some locations that had been given to cities. He
claimed, for example, that Ar Moab is not to be sought in
the place of the present-day Rabba. Mere hypotheses, such
as that Kirjathaim was another name for the principal city
of Moab, were given up.

The Seventh Edition was published in 1868. It contained
few changes from the former edition. More changes were
made in etymology, for instance, in the articles: רז - ערבה
צלצה. Other changes were made in primary meanings, and
then many corrections were made in citations and other
matters.

In appraising Dietrich's work in these three editions of
the lexicon, due credit must be given him for the excellent
contributions which he made to the study of Hebrew usage
and etymology. He took up the work where Gesenius had
left it, and he brought it nearer to completion. At the
same time it must not be overlooked that he also made
many combinations which were altogether too subtle and
uncertain. He also should have allowed himself more divisions of roots, according to the comparisons of the sister
tongues. Fortunately, he gave up most of the Indo-Germanic
comparisons, seeing that the comparative study of these languages was still at such an undeveloped stage, that the results
were far too uncertain to merit inclusion in a lexicon of
this kind. A close study of them would only have harmed
the more necessary study of the Hebrew and its kindred
dialects.

Dietrich increased the Arabic comparisons noticeably. He
was a good Arabist, and as Gesenius, he realized how valuable Arabic is for the study of Hebrew lexicography. But
it can hardly be denied that Dietrich quite often went too
far in the use of the Arabic, and took from it some very
uncertain primary meanings for the Hebrew. In his last
edition of the Manual, Gesenius had laid more emphasis on
Arabic than in his first editions. It was Dietrich who made

an overemphasis clearly perceptible. Both Gesenius and Dietrich gave as the primary meaning of: שָׁקַר *to color the truth,* according to the Arabic: *to be red.* Dietrich gave to: פָּדַר *to be fat,* the primary meaning: *to be weak, to break,* according to the Arabic comparison, while Ges. Ed. 4. gave: *to feed,* according to another Arabic comparison. From the Arabic, Dietrich introduced the primary meaning: *to wail* (*jammern*), for the root: אָבַל *to mourn, to be mournful.* Many of these primary meanings were just as uncertain as any that had been offered by Schultens or Michaelis.

The system of brackets which Dietrich used made it possible to compare his materials with those of Gesenius. This is profitable, inasmuch as frequently two opposing views stand side by side. However, the brackets hindered Dietrich from exercising the freedom that was necessary. A new etymology or primary meaning could quite easily be added, but this often necessitated a rearrangement which could not be carried out without revising the entire article.

While it is true that Dietrich contributed much to etymology, he neglected to bring in the new material which others had contributed, especially on the study of the meanings of words in special passages. It was unfortunate that the exegesis of Franz Delitzsch, based on the work of Fleischer, was practically disregarded, as was also some other important material in the commentaries of other scholars.

CHAPTER IV

MÜHLAU AND VOLCK

From Dietrich the editorship of the lexicon passed on to two men: F. Muehlau and W. Volck. The former was born in Dresden, June 20, 1839; the latter at Nueremberg. Both of them studied at the universities of Erlangen and Leipzig. And they claimed to be of the same philological school, a school that was not hostile to that of Gesenius, but in general in agreement with it.[1]

The editors based their etymology on the work of Fleischer which had gone over, to a great extent, into the commentaries of Franz Delitzsch. Fleischer's method was to determine the primary meaning of a word by going back to the original sensuous meaning. This original meaning may be found sometimes in the verb-stem, sometimes in appellatives, and sometimes only in the related stems of the cognate languages. In every case this primary meaning is to be sought, and upon it the secondary meanings are to be built, as they developed according to the psychology of the Semitic mind. Gesenius, as we have seen, made a special effort to find these fundamental meanings, but he was quite careful not to take them too quickly from the Arabic.

Dietrich's desire to retain Gesenius' literary character in the lexicon was abandoned. In the first place there was too much new material to be included, which could not well be done with the system of brackets. In the second place, the editors disagreed with Gesenius in Biblical-theological questions. In details they sometimes differed from one another. Where this was the case, both views had to be presented. In this way: עבד יי and כרוב were completely re-

---

[1] Cf. Introduction to Ges., Ed. 8.

vised, and to the latter were given as many as seven different etymologies.

Muehlau and Volck edited the 8.-11. editions of the Manual Lexicon. The first two of these editions still bear the old title: *Wilhelm Gesenius' Hebraeisches und Chaldaeisches Handwoerterbuch ueber das Alte Testament,* while the last two are entitled more exactly: *Wilhelm Gesenius' Hebraeisches und Aramaeischer Handwoerterbuch.*

The Eighth Edition was issued in 1878. It is practically of the same size as the former edition, but, due to a better German print and a smaller Arabic type, contains much more material. As before, the verbal-stems are printed in heavy type. In this edition a further improvement was made by giving to those stems which occur only in derivations an asterisk and no vowels. This is also done to nouns which do not occur in the absolute form.

The editors made the attempt, more thoroughly than had been done before, to trace all triliteral words to biliteral words whose meanings are primary. In order to avoid unnecessary repetition, they discussed all the derived roots in conjunction with the ע - ע root, which they considered the simplest expression of the root. We may illustrate their method by several examples. The root: בד and its derivatives were discussed under: בדד; the root מר under מרר. Ges. in 4. Edition and Dietrich's discussion of this root read as follows: It means: (1) *detach, separate, divide* (as in Arab.). The primary meaning: *to cut, to separate, divide,* is found with many modifications, partly in the one-syllable root: בד partly in the related roots with a harder pronunciation: cf. בת - פד - פת - בדל - בדק - בתת - - בתל - בתר - בתק - בדר - פרה - פתת - פתח - פתר . Related are the roots: בזז cf. בז - בץ - פץ. Thence: בד *part, member, branch,* etc. The etymological part of this article in Ges. Ed. 8. reads: בדר root: belongs to a numerous group of related roots, which are composed of a ב or פ and a labial (t or s) (cf. Philippi, in Morg. Forsch, Lpz. 1875, 101), and have the primary meaning: *to separate, divide.* To the root: בד belong besides: בדד also בדא - בדל - בדק - בדד - בעד - אבר cf. the Arab.: بع *to spread the legs,* بدو بدو بدا , بدر بده بعد باد . اٌبد . In the article: מרר Dietrich had the insertion: מרר related to: מרא - מרה - מור lit. *stringere,*

64 THE INFLUENCE OF GESENIUS

especially in the sense of drawing together, *to twist, wind, bind,* as we see in the III, VI, and IV conjugation of the Arabic word: مَرَّ *to wrestle with someone,* also found in:

مَرِيرَة *cord, rope:* στραγγάλη and in: מַר *drop,* στράγξ (lit. *something pressed out*). From: *to twist, to wind oneself* the Semitic notion of locomotion was developed, e. g., of water, which proceeds with a whirling motion. Ges. Ed. 8. maintained that the root was derived from: מַר from which root fourteen other Hebrew roots descended (which are enumerated), and besides these, twenty-four Arabic roots (which are also enumerated). Of all of these roots, Hebrew and Arabic, only two were given as doubtful. From this root, which received the primary meaning: *stringere, to stroke, to streak, to rub,* etc., the editors developed such diverse meanings as: *to stroke, to pluck, to make smooth, to be weak, sick, to hurry, run, proceed forward, to be tight, taut, to be strong, to be thick, to be bitter.* These illustrations show what was done to roots of this nature. A systematic attempt was made to reduce them all, that is, each separate group, to one biliteral root with only one primary meaning. Exceptions were, for example, גדד and מלל to which they gave more than one primary notion, and for which they accepted the existence of homonyms.

Besides these etymological changes, the editors dropped many roots which had been given to proper-nouns. Some of these were: אזק - אהד - אהר - אבץ. Dietrich and Gesenius gave to: אבץ a city in Isachar, the root: אבץ which had served no purpose. The editors of Ges. Ed. 8. leave the etymology undetermined. To the proper-name: אהוד the root: אהד *to be mild* had been given, according to the Arabic. The editors say that this root is doubtful. Likewise: אהר for: אחרון was given up.

On the other hand, the editors inserted new roots which were deemed necessary. Some of these were: אפע - אמה - אחה - אחזה. אחה was considered to be the root for: אח *brother,* but the editors refrained from giving a meaning. Dietrich had not recorded this root, but Gesenius gave it in his Thesaurus, and connected it with the Arabic root: *to be a friend.* However, he considered it to be a denominative. אמה *maidservant* was now derived from: אמה. Dietrich considered this root to be a denominative. אפע is given as the root of the word: אפע *nothingness (Nichtigkeit).*

A number of verb-stems were split into etymologically distinct stems. Some of these were: חבב - אנה - אלל - אוה - אהל The editors distinguished two roots אהל, one with the meaning: *to glitter*, based on the root: הל ; the other, a denominotive of: אהל. In this way they improved upon Gesenius' and Dietrich's treatment of this root. The former attempted to derive *tent* from the primary notion: *to glitter*, by saying that it glittered in the distance, while Dietrich added the remark that the notion *to glitter* had something in common with a thin substance such as cloth. The editors of Ges. Ed. 8. also distinguished three roots אוה : I. from the root: אן with the primary meanings *to bellow, howl, bleet*, and *bark;* II. analogous to the Arab. root: اوى *to go somewhere, to dwell there, turn to someone for shelter*: III. *to designate. mark*, a denominative of: אות. Ges. in Ed. 4. had recognized three different roots. Dietrich in Ges. Ed. 7. joined them all on the basis of the primary meaning: *to desire*. The editors of Ges. Ed. 8. recognized two roots אלל, one with the primary meaning: *to coalesce (coaluit)*; the other, *to whimper*. Ges. in Ed. 4. distinguished three roots, while Dietrich revised the entire article on the basis of the primary meanings: *to wind, to writhe*. Buhl in Ges. Ed. 17. now gives the primary meaning: *to be weak*.

The editors separated some roots, others, again, they joined. Some examples of the latter are: זרח - זלל - זכך. Let us note how they established an inner connection. The editors of Ges. Ed. 8. derived the root: זכך from זך cf. Arabic: زك دك and the Aram.: זך and דך. They gave the primary meaning as: *to pierce*, and from this they developed: *to dazzle the eye (in die Augen stechen)* and: *to be pure*. Dietrich in Ges. Ed. 7. had two roots: I. *to be sharp*, Arab. ذكا ; II. *to be blameless*, Arab. زكا while Ges. 4. had one root with the primary meaning: *to be pure*. The editors of Ges. Ed. 8. gave to: זלל the primary meaning: *to hang loosely*, and, from this they developed: *to flow down, to sway, to tremble*. The noun: *glutton* was developed by saying that he is one who causes food to slide down, cf. Arab. زلّ IV. Ges. in Ed. 4. had recognized only one root, while Dietrich gave two: I. *to be low;* II. *to tremble*.

The editors made changes not only in verb-stems, but

also in derived nominal stems. Many wrong orthographies
had to be corrected; new articles inserted; others dropped.
Some nominal forms had to be separated; others joined. To
others a new fundamental meaning was given. Although a
great deal was done for the study of the substantives, the
editors admit that much still remained, also, with regard to
the proper-names.

Some of the articles on the particles were worked over:
for example: בְּ and: כְּ. This was done on the basis of
Gesenius' Thesaurus. The meanings of: בְּ were arranged
more logically than they had been. The derivation of this
particle from: בֵּין or בַּיִת was given up. The editors said
that: בְּ (Arab. ب) should be compared with the Arab. في
its weaker form, Boettcher I, 337. They also gave up the
idea that: בְּ can be used interchangeably with: כַּאֲשֶׁר and
is used as a conjunction in certain passages, e. g., Isa. 8, 23
cf. 61, 11. They say that it is here used either adverbially
or attributively.[2] The particle כְּ they said, is not a preposition, but as Fleischer and Boettcher showed, a formally
undeveloped particle, and, as the Latin: *instar,* is used with
all cases. The editors found in the particle: כְּ the same
kaph demonstrative that we have in: כֹּה and in the personal pronouns, where it interchanges with: ת in the second person. The revision of the particles was also not very
thorough.

In this edition, Assyrian is used for the study of Hebrew
etymology for the first time. The editors admit that this
language had now been acknowledged to be grammatically
and lexicographically Semitic. In this edition it was introduced mainly to explain proper-names that had formerly
been explained from the Persian, e. g., Pul, Esarhaddon, and
Nebuchadrezzar. The first half of the name: Evil Merodach
is still suspected of having something in common with the
Hebrew word: *foolish.* Friedrich Delitzsch verified all the
Assyrian material that was introduced.

The editors attempted to eliminate all the Indo-Germanic
comparisons that remained. Although they recognized that
some progress had been made in the study of these comparisons, the results were still too uncertain to be used in
the lexicon.

---

[2] Delitzsch, Franz, Pss., Ed. 3, I, 313.

Articles dealing with geography and history were also revised. Of these, Muehlau, no doubt, contributed mostly to the study of geography, having helped with articles of this kind in Riehm's *Handwoerterbuch des biblischen Altertums,* while Volck made corrections in the historical matters, on the basis of what he had contributed to the second edition of: *Realencyclopaedie fuer protestantische Theologie und Kirche.*[3]

A disadvantage that the editors had to cope with in the preparation of this lexicon, was that it had to be re-edited in a limited time. Many matters could therefore not be revised as thoroughly as they should have liked to revise them. The essay on the sources of Hebrew philology remained untouched.

The Ninth Edition of the lexicon was published by Muehlau and Volck, in 1883, five years after the publication of the Eighth.

In this new revision the editors continued to make more corrections and changes in etymological materials. They eliminated some of the faulty etymologies found in the former editions. The permutation of the consonants in the Hebrew and related dialects was further studied, and illustrated by more examples. More Assyrian material was brought in, especially for the elucidation of proper-names. The editors did not risk the disturbance of time-honored etymologies until further Assyrian lexicographical studies should appear to verify the new material. In historical and archaeological articles the materials derived from the cuneiform were used more extensively.

With the aid of the concordances the completeness of the citations was tested, and the number of proof-texts was increased. Those articles in which all the references had been noted according to the number of times that the word occurs in the Old Testament, were marked with a cross at the end. This was a noteworthy innovation. The editors also attempted to make the list of the proper-nouns complete.

In exegetical matters, Delitzsch's commentaries were again used more extensively than those of the other commentators. The editors recognized that these commen-

---

[3] Strack, *Neue Jahrbuecher fuer Philologie und Paedagogik,* 1879, 2. Abteilung, 424.

taries contained more materials for exegesis and etymology
than, for instance, the commentaries of Ewald, Hitzig, Hupfeld and Dillmann. At the same time they insisted that they
had used the latter adequately.

The Ninth Edition also presented a revision of the essay
on the sources of Hebrew philology, originally prepared by
Gesenius and subsequently corrected by Dietrich. An attempt was made to retain Gesenius' text as much as possible.
The analytical index was increased and corrected, while the
German index was revised. The Ethiopic was added to the
list of the alphabets at the beginning of the book.

The editors received contributions from many scholars,
notably from Fleischer and Franz Delitzsch, for the Arabic
and Hebrew respectively. Dr. D. H. Mueller revised the
articles dealing with South Arabic words, and Schrader allowed them to use the manuscript of his second edition of:
Die Keilinschriften und das Alte Testament, before it had
been published. Besides these contributions, numerous reviews of the preceding edition were at the disposal of the
editors.

Of all the lexicons discussed so far, the eighth and ninth
editions of the Manual, prepared by Muehlau and Volck were
most severely criticized. The Eighth Edition was reviewed
rather leniently by E. Kautzsch;[4] but he did not fail to state
some of its shortcomings. In the meeting of the Interna-
tional Oriental Congress, September, 1881, dissatisfaction
was expressed concerning the lexicon. Barth charged the
editors with a too exclusive use of Delitzsch's commentaries, a mechanical use of the Arabic, and the elimination of valuable explanations for inferior ones. Fraenkel
criticized the phonology and the failure to distinguish between original words and words that had come into the
Arabic from the Aramaic. Nevertheless, the editors failed to
take the cue, and published the Ninth Edition in a manner
that was just as unsatisfactory as the Eighth. The result
was that C. Siegfried[5] and De Lagarde[6] criticized the editors
in scathing terms. McCurdy's review,[7] although more mod-
erate in tone, did not fail to state the demerits of the lexicon;

[4] Kautzsch, E., *Theo. Literaturzeitung,* 1878, 433 ff.
[5] *Theo. Literaturzeitung,* 1883, 529 f.
[6] *Goettinger G. A.,* 1884, 257 ff.
[7] *American Journal of Philology,* 1883, 343 ff.

while Friedrich Delitzsch also subjected it to a very careful scrutiny.[8] The consensus of opinion was that the lexicon showed: (1) The lack of a thorough and rational theory of the constitution of Semitic roots and the characteristic principles of Semitic phonology; (2) the want of a consistent etymological and philological method; (3) a failure to use adequately the exegetical and philological works of others besides those of Franz Delitzsch; and (4) a lack of direct controlling acquaintance with some of the most important Semitic dialects, notably of the Assyrian.

The editors correctly recognized the principle that many strong word-stems whose first consonants are the same, as for instance, the two consonants: דך show shadings of the same primary meaning; also that many weak word-stems, with the same strong radicals, as: צרר and צור may show different developments of the same fundamental motion. Gesenius had worked with this principle from the very beginning. He found the primary notion in the first two radicals of the strong root, as a rule, while Fuerst, later, looked for it in the last two. For instance, in the root: צמח Fuerst made the division צ and מח . Muehlau and Volck proceeded to carry out Gesenius' principle too consistently. They failed to note that there were a great number of strong word-stems which have the first two radicals in common, but display meanings that cannot be harmonized. Such are, for example: פתח to open, פתל to turn, פרר to break to pieces, and: פאר to decorate. The editors, failing to take note of this, brought together into groups all these seemingly related stems, and allowed them in most cases only one primary meaning. The result was that they brought together roots which were not in any way related to one another, just as if one should indiscriminately place together in English, the words: creek, crack, croon, crawl, crane, and creep, and say that they must have a fundamental meaning in common, since their first two radicals agree. The long series of roots which the editors grouped together in connection with the reduplicated root were therefore just so much worthless ballast; as they failed to show whether

[8] *Prolegomena*, 1886.
[9] Delitzsch, Friedr., *op. cit.*, 188 f.

70   THE INFLUENCE OF GESENIUS

these words were related or not, and made no distinction
between doubtful and ascertained cases, even listing words
that do not exist at all.

Since they had no consistent theory on the lengthening of
biliterals into triliterals in the history of the language, they
reduced triliteral roots to biliterals in a most fanciful and
arbitrary fashion. In his review of the Eighth Edition,
Kautzsch had called their attention to their failure to state
these principles. The result was that they made mistakes
such as the following: The verb: כרת was derived from:
כת whereas the infixing of ר is very rare or unknown
in Hebrew; nor does the root: כת contain the notion: to
cut, but: to strike. There are a large number of roots containing kr as the main element, with the primary notion: to cut,
to divide.[10] The root: בהר was derived from: בה while
Levy[11] derived it just as confidently from: בר. דלק was
derived from דל and it was compared with: דלע-דלה דלל.
The editors of Ges. Ed. 9. gave to this root the primary
meanings: to be movable, to flicker, from which the meaning: to burn was derived. Levy,[12] with equal assurance referred it to the biliteral root: לק and compared it with:
לחק-לקק He gave to it the primary meaning: to lick. A
whole series of roots was combined, following Fleischer and
Delitzsch, [13] under חוה which has strong letters at the
beginning and at the end, with Waw in the middle, and
was derived from the biliteral root: חו whose alleged
meaning: to twist, cannot be proved.[14] שבל was derived
from: של. But n, s and t in Hebrew are often predetermin-
ates. For example, ש is prefixed with the meaning: to
make, as is seen in the root: שקל to make light.[15]

The result of this wrong method was that many words
received a primary meaning that was utterly false. Thus
the editors tell us that: לחח to be fresh, lit. means: to
shine; בכה to weep, lit., to split; ברה to eat, lit. to cut
in; רטט to be afraid, lit., to be stepped on.[16] Fanciful etymologies were given with great assurance. Thus father

[10] McCurdy, op. cit., 347.
[11] Neuhebraeisches u. chaldaeisches Woerterbuch, I, 197.
[12] Op. cit., I, 410.
[13] Delitzsch, Pss, 1850, II, 124, Anmerkung.
[14] McCurdy, op. cit., 347.
[15] Farbridge, M. H., Biblical and Semitic Symbolism, 1923, 91.
[16] Delitzsch, Friedrich, op. cit., 190.

was called *the begetter; mother,* the *one preceding;* and
son, the builder. Siegfried, who adduced these last examples, overwhelmed by this mass of speculation, scented
a difficulty, and asked whether these people built houses
before they had sons. The editors gave to a root a primary meaning, and then developed almost any meaning
they pleased from it. The root: אל was made to yield
both: *to be strong* and *to be weak.*[17] The word: דם *blood*
was derived from the primary meaning: *to be like.* The
problem was to bring these two ideas together. The editors
did it in the following manner. *To be like* is *to be level,*
that is, be level with the ground. Something is made level
with the ground by pressing together. The notion: *to be
dark* is related to: *to be thick, close.* Blood is something
that is dark and thick. With ease the editors go from *strok-
ing* to *wounding;* from *tough* to *tender;* from *strong* to *weak.*
And this was practiced by men, says De Lagarde, who had
learned that: הבין meant: *distinxit,* before it developed
into: *intellexit.*[18]

The root-theory was applied not only to roots of frequent
occurrence, but was used also to explain roots that occur
only once or twice, or are not found in the verbal form at
all. Thus the meaning: *to rule* was developed from the
root: שרר by giving it the primary meaning: *to cut, to
separate, to divide.* From the notion: *to separate* the editors
developed: *to strive, to fight;* and the notion in: *to rule*
was considered to be that of *dividing, ordering.* Delitzsch
has shown that according to the Assyrian the fundamental
meaning of this root is very likely: *to glitter.*[19]

By developing the meanings in this haphazard fashion,
the editors of Ges. Ed. 8. and 9. frequently violated Gesenius'
canon of giving to a word its exact equivalent in German.
And quite naturally the correct order in the development of
meanings was also disturbed.

Much new material was brought in from the cognate languages, especially from the Arabic; but it was not adequately
used to separate those roots which should have been separated according to the sister tongues.[20] The other dialects

---

[17] Cf. also the root: מרר.
[18] De Lagarde, *op. cit.,* 268.
[19] Delitzsch, Friedr., *op. cit.,* 92.
[20] Noeldeke, *ZDMG,* 40, 718.

besides the Arabic: Aramaic, New Hebrew, and the Assyrian were not used extensively enough, e. g., the editors did not avail themselves of nearly all of the Assyrian material that was at their disposal.

As De Lagarde and Siegfried had indicated in their reviews, the material outside of Franz Delitzsch's commentaries had been very scantily used in these two editions. In a lexicon of this kind, which Gesenius had from the beginning intended for the whole learned world, it was to be expected that the contributions to Semitic philology and exegesis should be impartially reproduced. It was not necessary that the editors should bind themselves to any critical theory whose correctness they doubted.

Whatever shortcoming the Ninth Edition of the lexicon may have displayed, McCurdy pronounced it to be the best Hebrew lexicon on the market, and advocated its speedy translation into English. He therefore considered it superior to the new edition of Fuerst's Lexicon, re-edited by Ryssel, in 1876, from which Fuerst's untenable material had to a great extent been removed, and which revealed many excellencies.

Muehlau and Volck prepared the Tenth Edition, and it was published in 1886. In this edition the editors once more corrected the Hebrew orthography on the basis of Baer's editions of the Massoretic Text. Many wrong spellings were removed. Fuerst's concordance was used to revise the citations, and to verify the articles marked with a cross to show that all the passages in which the form occurs had been cited.

The Aramaic articles were improved and increased with the aid of: Kautzsch's *Grammatik des Biblisch-Aramaeischen.* An innovation in this lexicon was that the accent was given in all those forms where it falls on the penult instead of on the ultimate. In the pausal forms the accent which they have in the connection in which they stand was indicated.

The editors admitted that they went too far in etymologizing in the two preceding editions. Hence they shortened the etymological sections. They dropped many of the unwarranted biliteral roots and many of their untenable comparisons with the cognate languages. But they did not give up the principle that these groups of roots are all developments from one root that is biliteral.

The article: מרר was reduced to one-half its former size. In it the comparison with the kindred dialects was given up entirely. The primary meaning now read: *to be bitter*, lit. *to contract the palate*. The biliteral root: כת for כרת was dropped; also, בה for: בהר - דל for דלק and שׁל for שׁבל Many untenable primary meanings were removed, e. g., *to split* for *to weap; to shine* for *to cry*. We note that the root: מר no longer yielded both *to be strong* and *to sick;* neither: אלל both: *to be strong* and *to be weak*.

But only some of the objectionable etymologies were removed, and many artificial primary meanings and their developments were retained. Thus the root: פסם was made to yield both: *to spread out* and *to cease*, although the dialects show that we have two roots. ברה *to eat*, was still derived from the ordinary meaning: *to cut in*. Thus the separation of roots according to the cognate tongues was still not carried out sufficiently well.[21] The editors continued to overstress the Arabic by giving to Hebrew roots untenable primary meanings. Thus Hebrew usage had to give place to the Arabic in the root: נהל which properly means: *to lead*, but here received the additional meaning: *to lead to a watering place*. Likewise: גלשׁ whose meaning according to Hebrew usage should be: *to hang down*, received the meaning: *to lie in a hanging position (herablagern)*, from the Arabic comparison: جلس *to sit*,[22] found in Franz Delitzsch's Commentary to Canticles.[22a] The primary meaning of: ידע *to place in the mind*, given in Ges. Ed. 8. and 9., was doubted in Ges. Ed. 10., because the dialects show an original Yad. In the article: מלך the Arabic influenced the editors to give this root the primary meaning: *to lay hold of, to grab;* whereas the comparison with the Assyrian shows that the primary meaning is: *to rule*, as Ges. Ed. 4. had it.

In another respect the comparisons with the dialects were improved. New material was introduced in Aramaic, Assyrian, and epigraphy. Dr. I. Loew contributed toward the Post-Biblical Hebrew and the Aramaic, while Friedrich De-

---

[21] Noeldeke, *ZDMG*, 40, 718.
[22] Delitzsch, Fried., *op. cit.*, 24.
[22a] *Biblischer Commentar ueber die poetischen Buecher des Alten Testaments*, 1875, IV, 66

litzsch again corrected the Assyrian material. The editors received most of their Assyrian material from the latter's: *The Hebrew Language Viewed in the Light of Assyrian Research,* 1883, but the *Prolegomena,* 1886, did not appear early enough for this edition.

The Assyrian material for the 10. Edition was used to explain not only proper-names, but also the names of months, certain plants, animals, and precious stones. We might consider just a few instances to see how the Assyrian was of value in the lexicon. The word: אֲנִי formerly compared with the Egyptian and the Arabic only, was now referred also to the Assyrian. The Assyrian substantiates the Semitic origin of the word. The editors of Ges. Ed. 10 added that the word: שֵׁבֶט *staff* is found in the Assyrian: sibtu and its verb: sabatu, *to strike,* but they still clung to their Arabic derivation: سبط *to be long.* The Assyrian also helped to explain certain roots that do not occur in the Kal form in the Hebrew. Thus the well-known Hebrew verb-form: הכלים formerly taken to be the Hiphil of the verb: כלם *to strike, to wound,* now was derived from the Assyrian: kalamu, *to shorten.* New primary meanings were taken over from the Assyrian. In Ges. Ed. 9, the Hebrew root: נבט had been explained by means of the Arabic: نبط *to spring forth,* as water. The Assyrian preserves the more original meaning: *to shine.* Most of the Assyrian was taken over from Delitzsch's book: *The Hebrew Language.* However, the editors did it hesitatingly. Although they admitted that they had gone too far in the use of the Arabic, they did not wish to substitute Assyrian material for it, of which they themselves were not sure. Much of the old untenable material was therefore retained together with the new explanation from the Assyrian.

Valuable epigraphic contributions were furnished for this edition by D. H. Mueller. Word-criticism and conjectural emendations received little more space than in the preceding editions. The editors did not consider it the duty of a lexicon to record all these. Archaeological and exegetical materials were revised more thoroughly in accordance with the newest discoveries, and the latest references were inserted in the essay on Hebrew philology. In matters pertaining to the history of religion the editors retained their

views, opposed quite often to those of Wellhausen, De Lagarde, and Siegfried.

The Eleventh Edition of the lexicon was published in
1890. This edition bears the more exact title: *Wilhelm Gesenius' Hebraeisches und Aramaeisches Handwoerterbuch
ueber das Alte Testament.* In this edition the editors made
no essential improvements over the preceding edition. A
few corrections and additions made a number of extra pages
necessary, otherwise it contains all the faults of the former
edition. The valuable article on: *The Sources of Hebrew
Lexicography,* found at the beginning of the lexicon, originally written by Gesenius, and later brought up to date by
the subsequent editors, was dropped from this edition. This
was not so unfortunate as it was so out-of-date that it was
well that it should be dropped until it could be thoroughly
revised.

The final edition of the Manual published by Muehlau and
Volck compares with the first lexicon published by Gesenius as follows: Hebrew and Aramaic were still intermin-
gled, although the arguments for a separation of the two had
been clearly and convincingly put forth. The old order of
discussing the proper-nouns in conjunction with the other
words of the lexicon and the arrangement of all the words
of the lexicon in the alphabetical order were retained
in spite of what such eminent scholars as Friedrich Delitzsch and Noeldeke had said to the contrary.[23] However,
the alphabetical arrangement of words had much to be said
in its favor. The editors changed the misnomer *Chaldaic* to
Aramaic on the title page and elsewhere. And finally, they
adhered to the empirical method of dealing with the Hebrew
Massoretic Text. As Gesenius they discussed only the most
necessary corrections, excluding most of the results of textual criticism.

With Muehlau and Volck as editors, sound progression in
etymology was very slight. Concerning their method, De
Lagarde said:[24]

The consistent manner in which Muehlau and Volck trace
all triliterals to biliterals, I should not criticise in itself.
Naturally many mistakes were made; but on the slippery

23 *ZDMG,* 40, 718; *Prolegomena,* 3 ff.
24 *Goettinger G. A.,* 1884, 267 f.

territory of etymology, as well as on most of the other terri-
tories of knowledge, one does not proceed in a straight line.

To this Friedrich Delitzsch correctly adds:[25] "Nevertheless it is a shame that the advance made on this precariously
crooked line does not amount to a hair-breadth." Manifestly
Muehlau and Volck hindered sound etymology by their unscientific method. Very obviously they lacked the lexicographical ability of Gesenius and Dietrich. They lacked the
clearness, force, and selective qualities of the former and the
philosophic insight of the latter. The result was: what Gesenius and Dietrich did slowly and painstakingly, although
not without mistakes, these editors attempted to do in such
a hasty and haphazard fashion that scholars had to voice a
violent protest. In the end, Muehlau and Volck were not
altogether to blame, as they had inherited many wrong
primary and developed meanings from Gesenius and Dietrich.

During the editorship of Muehlau and Volck the lexicon
lagged considerably in presenting the latest results of Semitic learning. They lacked a thorough knowledge of the cognate languages, especially of the Assyrian. They had to receive this material at second-hand. The new material coming in from the Assyrian was too much for these two men
to handle, as was the material coming in from other de-
partments of Semitics. They had charge of the publication
of the lexicon at a very critical time, and when we bear this
in mind, we get a more sympathetic understanding of the
difficulties they had to contend with.

Although the lexicon left the hands of Muehlau and Volck
in a most imperfect state, its popularity did not wane dis-
astrously. At that time there was only one lexicon in the
English and the German languages that approached it in
completeness, and that was Ryssel's edition of Fuerst's
lexicon, Ed. 1876. The fact that Gesenius' name was on the
title-page gave many the thought that the lexicon still maintained its standard of excellence.

---

[25] Delitzsch, Friedr., *op. cit.*, 189.

CHAPTER V

The Twelfth Edition of Gesenius' Manual Lexicon marked a new era in the history of lexicography. With it began the careful editorship of Frants Buhl, of Leipzig, now of Kopenhagen, and his two able assistants, Albert Socin and H. Zimmern. Buhl has the general knowledge of the Semitic languages, as well as the restraint and discrimination to qualify him as a lexicographer. The late Socin was an eminent Arabist, while Zimmern ranks with the foremost Assyriologists.

Six editions appeared with Buhl as editor. The lexicon appeared with the title: *Wilhelm Gesenius' Hebraeisches und Aramaeisches Handwoerterbuch ueber das Alte Testament in Verbindung mit Prof. Alb. Socin und Prof. H. Zimmern, bearbeitet von Dr. Frants Buhl, Leipzig,* 1895. The 13. Edition was published in 1899, under the same title. The 14. was issued in 1905 without the name of Socin, who had died, but with the assistance of Müller and Zimmern. Buhl prepared the Fifteenth with the assistance of Zimmern, W. Max Mueller, and O. Weber, in 1910. The Sixteenth appeared with the same group of editors, in 1915. All of these lexicons are careful revisions, one of the other, until we come to the last edition, the Seventeenth. This appeared as an anastatic reprint of the Sixteenth Edition, in 1921.

The Twelfth Edition represented a radical revision of the Eleventh in form as well as in content. For the first time the Biblical Aramaic was separated from the Hebrew. Scholars had long advocated this as the best arrangement. It had been adopted in Siegfried and Stade's Hebrew lexicon.[1] The German index was reintroduced, and instead of the ref-

---

[1] *Hebraeisches Woerterbuch zum Alten Testament,* 1892-93.

erences being given to the Hebrew lexicon proper, the
Hebrew equivalents were placed next to the German. This
was a distinct advantage, since it enabled the student to find
what he was looking for by one process, and it absolved
the editors from completely revising the citations for each
succeeding edition. F. O. Kramer, who took care of this part
of the lexicon, also improved the word-selection. In Ges.
Eds. 8. 9. 10. as high as 450 proper-names had been included
in the index. Among them there were words such as Gilgal,
Magog, and Absolom, for which one would hardly look in
the index.

In the lexicon proper, Socin took care of the comparative
material. In this revision he compared especially the Arabic
dialects, which he had mastered as few others had done.
The extent of Socin's contributions and their application are
not clearly defined. Zimmern dealt exclusively with the
Assyrian material. It was his intention to record only that
which possessed the greatest degree of reliability. He did
not pretend to be at all exhaustive in his contributions. To
complete the Phoenician parallels, Bloch's *Phoenizisches
Glossar*, 1891, was used. And for the South Arabic comparisons, the glossary of Hommel's Chrestomathy was compared,
otherwise the contributions of D. H. Mueller remained unchanged. The well-known studies of Barth and De Lagarde
in the formation of nouns were often cited, but we note
that Buhl did not unconditionally accept the views of either
of them.

The first thing that strikes our attention in the etymological portion of the lexicon is the uncertainty that still
obtained with regard to the etymology of many words. Siegfried called attention to the following examples:[2] No etymology was given to: אָב although a reference was made
to the various etymologies that had been attempted. Likewise: בֵּן - אָח - אֵם are without etymology. Uncertainty was
expressed with regard to: אָדוֹן although the current etymology was alluded to: דוּן - אָדֹן . The editors of Ges. Ed. 11.
had given this etymology as a matter of course. With regard to: אֵל the various etymologies were cited, but the
editor committed himself to none of them. The same was
true of the words: עָמִין - מִכְכַן - לֵוִי - אָגַן - אֱלוֹהַ.

Buhl, in Ges. Ed. 12 gave no etymology to the word: חָשַׁשׁ

---

[2] *Theo. Literaturzeitung*, 1895, 302 f.

hay, dry grass. Ges. Ed. 11. had derived it from the root
with the same radicals, and had begun with the primary
meaning: *to press together.* The root: רגם for: תרגם was
dropped. On the other hand: שמרה *eye-lid*, whose derivation from: שמר *to guard, to keep,* was doubted in Ges. Ed.
11. was accepted in Ges. Ed. 12. The root: דנג for: דונג
wax, was dropped. A systematic attempt was made to drop
all the uncertain etymologies given in the former edition,
and where nothing definite was found, the etymology was
simply omitted, or else a reference was made to the different suggestions of scholars.

Buhl in Ges. Ed. 12. dropped many of the primary meanings that are found in the preceding edition. Although
Gesenius' method of finding the primary meaning and then
arranging the developed meanings in logical order was
still followed, Buhl did not seek primary meanings, as his
predecessors had done. He gave the Hebrew word. First
in the article he placed the comparison with the dialects,
and then, the primary meaning which was found in the
Hebrew usage. Thus, Buhl in Ges. Ed. 12. treated the root:
נכה as follows. First, we find the comparison with the
dialects, and then, the first meaning, as it occurs in the
Hebrew, namely, the Niphal perf. *to be smitten.* The editors
of Ges. Ed. 11. referred us first to a number of related
Hebrew roots, and then told us that the primary meaning
was: *to thrust, to strike, to injure, to batter to pieces,* and
then the meanings which occur in the Old Testament followed together with their citation. In the same way, Buhl
in Ges. Ed. 12. dropped the primary meaning: *to thrust, to
drive,* in the article: דדה; *to cover up,* in: סגר; *stringere.
stroke,* etc., in the article: מרר *to be bitter.*

Many roots that had formerly been brought together as
related, by giving them a general primary meaning, were
separated again according to the different roots found in the
cognate languages. The editors of Ges. Ed. 11. gave one
root: זחל *to crawl,* and from this was derived: *to fear.*
Buhl in Ges. Ed. 12. gave two roots: I. *to crawl;* II. *to fear.*
The editors of Ges. Ed. 12. treated: ברה as one root: *to cut,*
from which was derived: *to eat.* Ges. Ed. 12. distinguished
two roots: I. *to cut;* II. *to eat.* On the other hand, where
Ges. Ed. 11. divided a root, Ges. Ed. 12. sometimes joined
it again. This was the case, for instance, in the article:

אוה while Ges. Ed. 11. distinguished three roots, Ges. Ed. 12. brought all the meanings together under one. Ges. Ed. 11. distinguished three roots אלה , Ges. Ed. 12. had only one.

The elimination of a great deal of unsound etymological material, as well as other unnecessary discussions, saved much space. In addition, the translations of proper names were dropped everywhere; Greek equivalents were added occasionally, and a reference to the Hebrew root was added where such could be made. This space was used to advantage by giving a better picture of the Hebrew language itself. Buhl increased the number of citations, and paid more attention to Hebrew constructions and quotations. The citations in more articles were completed, and at the end appeared the customary cross.

More thoroughly than had been done by Muehlau and Volck, Ges. Ed. 12. made use of the commentaries, monographs, and text-critical contributions. He introduced the critical views of scholars on the text. He called attention to many of the words of the Massoretic Text whose soundness had been questioned, and he added the proposed reading or a reference. For example, in connection with the difficult passage in 1 Sam. 17, 12, he made a reference to the proposed reading given in Driver's Samuel. But he failed to quote the proposed reading. This, of course, made it difficult for those students who were not in possession of the commentary to use it. The articles pertaining to the history of religion and Biblical theology were rewritten in accordance with the latest critical views. In these articles Buhl exhibited great skill in bringing together the different views within a very limited space. Articles of this kind were: אלה - תרפים - יהוה - אפוד . In the article: אפוד Buhl, unsuccessfully we believe, attempted to harmonize the two views that: אפוד meant both: *the garment of a priest* and *the statue of Jahve,* by saying that the latter might be a garment spread over a statue of this kind.

The general excellence of this, in many respects, new lexicon prepared by Buhl was immediately recognized. It was favorably reviewed by A. Bevan[3] and C. Siegfried.[4] It was imperative that the lexicon should maintain a high de-

³ *Critical Review,* 1895, 128 ff.
⁴ *Loc. cit.*

gree of excellence at this particular time. While Ges. Ed. 12.
was in preparation, Siegfried and Stade published their
Hebrew lexicon.[5] In this lexicon the editors made a greater
effort to bring out the meanings of Hebrew words in different passages. They increased the number of citations and
quotations. Their method was not to look for a primary
meaning in order to trace the developed meanings from this.
They contended that we are too far removed from the time
when this development occurred, if it did occur. They excluded from their lexicon the comparisons with the cognate
languages, with the exception of some references to where
this material might be found. The Biblical theology of this
lexicon was strongly influenced by the unsound theories of
these men. The fact that they omitted the comparisons with
the dialects offset the gain which they achieved by studying
the different constructions. The lexicon was favorably reviewed by Budde.[6] Buhl made use of the first half of this
lexicon. When the second half appeared, the purely lexicographical material of Buhl's lexicon was already in manuscript. The appearance of this lexicon very probably induced him to increase the number of citations in his lexicon.

The Thirteenth Edition was published in 1899. With this
edition the size of the volume began to increase again.
Three and a half sheets were added to the former edition.
These additions consisted in the increased number of citations and constructions as well as of references to the
recent material in exegesis, text-criticism, and philology.
There was a certain unevenness in the references to the
current literature as the printing of the book took an entire
year, and many articles could be used only for the second
part of the book.

The text and the arrangement were the same as in the
former edition. Both the 12th and the 13th Editions were
clear and legible. Numerous corrections were made in the
text of the lexicon, but not nearly so many as were necessary.
The articles marked with a cross were verified by means
of the Hebrew concordance of Mandelkern.

In this edition, the study of the gender of nouns was

---

[5] *Hebraeisches Woerterbuch zum Alten Testament,* 1892-93.
[6] *Theo. Literaturzeitung,* 1892, 58 ff.; 1894, 415 ff.

improved. The gender of a noun was given only when it
could be proved from constructions in which the word occurred. Such examples of construction were also the predi-
cate when it preceded the noun and was confirmed by other
cognate languages or other analogies. For the study of gender, Buhl made use of Albrecht's articles in *Zeitschrift fuer
alttestamentliche Wissenschaft*, 15. Examples of changes in
the gender of nouns may be noted in: תֵּימָן which Ges.
Ed. 12. had listed as masculine, with the exception of Ct.
4, 16, where he considered the word to be feminine. In
Ges. Ed. 13. it was considered only feminine. עִיר was considered to be of feminine gender in Ges. Ed. 12, with a
few exceptions; in Ges. Ed. 13. Buhl gave to it just the
feminine gender.

Buhl also made extensive use of the treatise: Gerber, *Die
hebraeischen Verba Denominativa*, 1896. It was cited in
many places where Buhl considered the material to be convincing or noteworthy. Buhl said that he agreed with
Gerber in this that many more verbal-stems were denominatives, than had been ordinarily supposed. The arrangement
of words in the lexicon, consisting namely of verbs and
nouns derived from them, is often merely a matter of convenience. Buhl did not believe that all of the derived
meanings are denominatives. The matter was too uncertain to rearrange the lexicon in accordance with this theory.
A reference to Gerber was made, for example, in the article
רָעָה II, Buhl added that Gerber considered the perf. Kal
No. 1, Piel, and Hithpael to be denominatives of: רַע .

In Ges. Ed. 12. numerous citations were taken from the
certified portions of the recently discovered Hebrew text of
Sirach. The Phonician parallels were given from Bloch's
Glossar, and the Ancient Aramaic, Nabataean, and Pal-
myrene material was quoted from the texts themselves. The
contributions of D. H. Mueller, whose retention in the former
edition had caused both the editor and the publisher some
trouble, were dropped altogether in this edition. Thus, for
example, Mueller's theory concerning the origin of the word:
אִיזֶבֶל was eliminated. Instead the results of Hommel's labors
were inserted in this article as in the article: אִיכָבוֹד . Likewise other material that had been introduced in Ges. Ed. 12.
was dropped again, for example, Winckler's hypothesis on:
חֶלְאָה He had suggested the emendation to: בְּלַח . Ges. Ed.

12. recognized the M. T. to be sound, and said it was the *halahha* of the cuneiform tablets.

To give a thorough survey of the changes that were made from time to time in the different articles would be impossible. A few illustrations must suffice to show the attention that was given to detail. In the article: I אלה Ges. Ed. 12. referred to the Assyrian infinitive: utallu, *to ban, to swear;* sutelu, *to swear.* This was dropped in Ges. Ed. 13. In the article: אלה II a printer's error was corrected, and the Assyrian comparison: ulu, *cry of pain* and: allu, *woe,* were dropped. In the article: אלה I a reference to Gerber was added. And for the reference to Wellhausen's *Skizzen,* his *Reste des arabischen Heidentums* was substituted. The meanings of the Kal of אלה I were slightly changed, and another emendation was added to 1 Kg. 8, 31. In the article: רכל the missing citation Nah. 3, 16 was added in Ges. Ed. 13, and the vowels were given to Cornill's emendation to Ez. 27, 24. The articles: מרץ - מרפא - רם - II - I on the other hand were left exactly as they were in the former edition.

As in Ges. Ed. 12., the proper-names were not translated. The editor maintained that the South Arabic studies presented too many new problems. But some of the Septuagint renderings were given. A reviewer suggested that it would have been worth while to give the cuneiform equivalents for exilic names also.[7]

The lexicon was favorably reviewed by Felix Perles,[8] Dr. R. Z.,[9] and Fr. Schwally.[10] Each of these reviewers added a list of corrections and proposed changes. Felix Perles praised the lexicon in the following words:[11]

No work is beter calculated to give a vivid impression of the progress made in the knowledge of the Old Testament than the new edition of Gesenius' dictionary, which has just made its appearance. During the four years which have elapsed since the publication of the previous edition, our knowledge of the Hebrew language has been increased to an unusual degree by numerous grammatical, philological, critical, and exegetical writings. The constantly growing litera-

---

[7] R. Z. *Theo. Literaturblatt,* 1900, 52 f.
[8] *JQR,* 1899, 688 f.
[9] *Theo. Literaturblatt,* 1900, 52 f.
[10] *Theo. Literaturzeitung,* 1899, 355 f.
[11] *Op. cit.,* 688.

ture, often inaccessible and scattered over various period-
icals, makes it imperative that a compendious collection be
made of the results achieved to serve the student as a reli-
able guide. This would require a high degree of self-denial
and untold labor, and we cannot be sufficiently grateful to
Buhl and his co-workers for the scrupulous care and conscientiousness with which they have worked and critically
utilized the results of the numerous separate inquiries in the
field of lexicography. They have created a veritable reper-
toire and an indispensable reference-book for the study of
the Old Testament.

The Fourteenth Edition was published in 1905. Although
the lexicon was smaller in compass by six sheets than the
previous edition, it contained additional material. This was
accomplished by widening the columns, reducing the size
of the print, and by introducing a briefer system of abbreviation. The comparative and etymological material was
now given in smaller print than the lexicographical material. This not only saved space, but enabled one to glance
through the articles much faster.

The contents and text of the lexicon underwent considerable change. Previously, Buhl had attempted to treat the
text of the lexicon as conservatively as possible, so as to
retain its original character. The result was that he often
sponsored opinions which in reality were not his, but he
could not exactly prove their untenability. In this edition
the editor rearranged the lexicographical material, especially in the longer articles.

As before, Zimmern took care of the Assyrian comparisons. His painstaking hand is everywhere in evidence. He
also contributed notes on other matters. For the first time
a specialist in Ancient Egyptian was added to the staff,
namely, W. Max Mueller. A new system for the translitera-
tion of the Egyptian and Coptic words was introduced.
Mueller's contributions were marked with his signature. He
endeavored to give, as briefly as possible, the loan-words
from the Egyptian in the Palestinian Semitic and vice versa.
Words whose relationship went back to very ancient times
were not included.

Buhl treated the proper-names as before. A majority of
them he referred to monographs on the subject. In addition
to the works of Nestle, Buchanan Gray, Gerber, and Grun-
wald, he called attention to the article: *Names,* in the Ency-

clopaedia Biblica and to Lidzbarski's article on: *Semitische Kosenamen*, in the second volume of his *Ephemeris*, 1 ff. He used Noeldeke's contributions to proper-names in his *Beitraege zur semitischen Sprachwissenschaft* only for the second part of the lexicon.

The suggestion had been offered to include words that had been arrived at by conjecture, in the Lexicon. But the editor felt that this should not be done in the lexicon proper. The difficulty in selecting those words which should be included and those which should be excluded would be too great. To comply partly with the wish of those who had made this suggestion, Buhl added a small list of words arrived at by conjecture, at the end of the lexicon.

The editor made use of the reviews of the previous edition, and received numerous contributions from the outside. Paul Haupt helped him with the literature published in America.

This edition was reviewed very favorably by Eduard Koenig.[12] He commended Buhl for explaining Hebrew ideas from Hebrew antiquity itself, instead of adopting the explanations offered by the Pan-Babylonists. As example, Koenig cited: רקיע which Buhl translated: *the solid expanse of the firmament (die feste Himmelswoelbung)* (LXX: στερέωμα , Jerome, *firmamentum*); not: *zodiac*, as the Babylonists would have it. Likewise: ברית is translated: *treaty, alliance*, followed by the derived meanings: *covenant with a pledge, divine promise*, as Koenig had shown in his: *Hauptprobleme der altisraelischen Religionsgeschichte*, p. 84. Koenig also defended this view over against Wellhausen and Stade in his: *Offenbarungsbegriff des Alten Testament* II, 338-40. In general, Koenig commended the impartial manner in which Buhl presented the different views of the critics.

The Fifteenth Edition of the lexicon was published in 1910. It was not so great a revision of the preceding edition as the Fourteenth was of the Thirteenth. The additional material of four and a half sheets consists mainly in recording the latest literature on lexicography. The most noteworthy of the new material was taken from the Jewish papyri found in Egypt, Brockelmann's *Vergleichende Gram-*

---

[12] *Theo. Literaturblatt*, 1905, 451.

matik, Smend's studies in the Hebrew text of Sirach, and the results of Musil's travels.

The text of the lexicon was even more compressed than it had been in the former edition. Long articles that had formerly been divided into several paragraphs marked by indentation are given in continuous print. For instance, in Ges. Ed. 9, the article: עַל had been divided into thirteen indented paragraphs. In Ges. Ed. 14. these had been reduced to eight. In this edition there were only four. As many as five columns, one after the other, were presented without any indentation. This made it very difficult to pick out the divisions, although they are marked by means of letters of the alphabet and numerals.

In this edition there was an increase in the number of grammatical forms added to the verb. In Ges. Ed. 9 פָּעַל - יִפְעַל and once with *o,* in Job 35, 6 were listed. In Ges. Ed. 14, nine forms were listed; and in Ges. Ed. 15., there were fourteen. Two forms were still missing to make the number of forms that occur complete, namely, פְּעַלְתִּי and תִּפְעַל But to record all these regular forms of the verb is not the work of the lexicon, but of the concordance.[13] The list of words arrived at by conjecture, given at the end of the lexicon, was almost doubled in this edition.

Zimmern again took care of the Assyrian material, and W. Max Mueller, of the Egyptian. As in the former edition, he omitted the loan-words of very ancient origin, in order not to be compelled to bring in a comparison of the Hamitic also. O. Weber compared the Old South Arabic material insofar as it touched upon the Ancient Hebrew. With the addition of Weber to the staff, the comparative material of the lexicon reached a high stage of development. This edition of the lexicon was published practically a 100 years after Gesenius had published his first lexicon. Then the study of modern Hebrew lexicography was still in its initial stages, carried on mostly along traditional lines. Practically nothing was known of Egyptian, Assyro-Babylonian, and South Arabic antiquity. The lexicon represented an epitome of the extent of the labor that had been bestowed on the entire province since that time. The progress is seen not only in the comparison of this edition with the edition of

---

[13] Ralfs, *Theo. Literaturzeitung,* 1911, 4.

1810-12, but also with the edition of five years before, over which, on its external side it showed an increase of fifty pages.[14]

The Sixteenth Edition of the lexicon was published in 1915. Since the 17., printed in 1921, is an anastatic reprint of this edition, the 16. is the final revision. In the preface, Buhl tells us why he did not consider a radical rearrangement in the form of the lexicon. He expected this to be the last edition which he would edit. He, therefore, did not undertake the alphabetical order of roots or the edition of two lexicons: a thesaurus and a manual. The latter suggestion, although attractive, did not appeal to Buhl. As the lexicon is constituted now, it can be published at regular intervals, with its material brought up to date. In case it should be printed both as a thesaurus and a manual, the thesaurus would not be printed often enough. Its material would always be in arrears, and exploded theories would receive a sort of canonization which they do not deserve. In the meantime, scholars would have to spend their time looking for material scattered in magazine articles and monographs. A supplementary pamphlet issued from time to time would not be very convenient either.

Gesenius' Manual Lexicon therefore remained what it had naturally grown to be, strictly speaking, neither a thesaurus nor a manual lexicon. As a thesaurus it has not enough detail. The numerous lexical, textcritical and exegetical notes can often only be referred to, instead of being quoted. Often Buhl must refrain from giving a definite decision of his own because space keeps him from bringing out the arguments for both sides of the case with sufficient detail. As a manual lexicon the book contains too much material. Much of the comparative material, as well as the references to current literature could be abbreviated or else omitted. The lexicographical material could then be grouped in a manner that would facilitate reference. In its present state, it is very difficult to glance through the articles.

This edition was reviewed by Fr. Schwally,[15] F. Perles,[16] and Caspari.[17] Schwally's objection was that the lexicon

---

[14] Perles, *JQR, New Series*, 2, 97.
[15] *Theo. Literaturblatt*, 1916, 26 ff.
[16] *JQR*, 1916, 79 f.
[17] *Theo. Literaturblatt*, 1915, 488 f.

carried with it too much unnecessary ballast in etymology
and philology, too many untenable suppositions of the
critics; and he would have omitted the notes on pp. xiv-xix
altogether. Both Schwally and Perles would study the Hebrew usage more than had been done. They added numerous textual, philological, and lexicographical suggestions.
Caspari criticized the arrangement of some of the meanings.
Of course, he admitted that the ideal arrangement according to the development of the Hebrew word can often not
be attained due to our imperfect knowledge of its very ancient development; but many of the meanings could be
arranged more logically. He cited, for example, the word:
כבוד. In arranging the meanings, Buhl in Ges. Ed. 16. began with the moral concept: 1. *Honor (Ehre)*. This was
followed by the material concept: 2. *wage of honor,
wage (Ehrensold, Lohn)*. Then follow: 3. *that by which
one seeks honor (das, worin man seine Ehre sucht)*;
4. *glory, splendor*, e. g., of a kingdom; 5. *the glory of
God;* 6. *glory as an epithet of the soul*. To obtain a more
logical arrangement, Caspari would place 3 and 1 together;
2 with 4; make 5 a special case of 4; and make 6 a special
case of 1 or 4. Number 6 he says, is the majesty of the
king praying in the Psalms, and the attempt should not be
made to derive the word in this last case from a separate
etymology. Caspari also called attention to the fact that the
German equivalents for Hebrew words were often not so
exact as they should be. To illustrate this, he adduced several examples from Genesis 40. פרח should be translated:
to bud (ausschlagen), not: *to sprout (sprossen)*. Ges. Ed.
16. gave this more exact equivalent in the German index.
Caspari would translate the Hiphil: השביל more accurately:
put forth (treiben), instead of: *to ripen (reifen)*. ענב
is properly the grape-berry, and should therefore be translated: *berry (Beere)*, not just: *grape (Traube)*. שחט should
be rendered: *to squash (quetschen)*, not: *to squeeze-out
(ausdruecken)*. In this respect the lexicon is still in need
of considerable improvement, as we shall see when we
come to speak of Delitzsch's criticism.

The reviews of Ges. Ed. 16. were more detailed than
those of some of the previous editions. But it remained for
Friedrich Delitzsch to study the lexicon thoroughly and to
give his observations. The great service which this late

Assyrian scholar has rendered to Hebrew lexicography must not be overlooked. In his: *Hebrew Language Viewed in the Light of Assyrian Research,* and also in his: *Prolegomena,* he had made valuable contributions to Hebrew lexicography, although he did not escape the just criticism that he had overemphasized the Assyrian.[18] After using the lexicon for a longer period than 30 years, from the Eighth Edition upward he again ventured to give his criticism.[19] This criticism he extended also to Koenig's *Hebraeisches und Aramaeisches Woerterbuch zum Alten Testament,* 1900, and to the English Gesenius by Brown, Driver, and Briggs. We can consider the review only in its broader phases.

Delitzsch was glad that his suggestion to separate the Hebrew from the Biblical Aramaic had finally been adopted. However, he deplored the fact that the editor did not yet see fit to separate the proper-nouns from the other words. Delitzsch had offered some very cogent reasons why these two suggestions should be adopted.[20] He said that the usual reason for retaining the alphabetical order was not as convincing as it appeared to be, since there are only about thirty words whose etymology is uncertain. These could be placed in their regular alphabetical order.

The next criticism was that many roots were given in the lexicon which cannot actually be proved to exist in the Hebrew.[21] He ventured to say that there are as many as forty such roots. As wrong he designated: קיץ which was said to exist by the side of: יקץ He maintained that some forms of יקץ accidentally followed the paradigm of: קים but this did not mean that these forms must originally have followed the latter paradigm. Many of these roots which should not be in a lexicon, were based on *matres lectiones* which were added later, and obscured the original character of the root. He would admit only the root: משש not either: מוש or: ימש He said that the latter roots are no more entitled to existence than the root: נשה is on the basis of the form: נשוי in Ps. 22, 1.

His next criticism of the lexicon was that the different meanings and shadings of meaning should be brought out

---

[18] Noeldeke, *ZDMG*, 1886, 718.
[19] *Orientalistische Literaturzeitung*, 1916, 162 ff.; 193 ff.
[20] *Ibidem*, 163.
[21] *Ibidem*, 164 ff.

more exactly in the German. To illustrate this, he cited
the following words. רעף should mean: *to drip* (*triefen*),
not: *to trickle* (*traeufeln*). Koenig and BDB[22] have both:
to trickle and *to drip*. ערף I and פרם properly mean: *to
break in two, divide* (*teilen*), as BDB and not: *to break*
(*brechen*). טמן means: *to bury* (*verscharren*) and not
just: *to hide, to conceal* (BDB), Ges. Ed. 16: *verbergen*, bes.
verscharren. דעך means originally: *to cease glowing, to
cool down* (*verglimmen*), not: *to be extinguished* (BDB,
Koenig, and Ges. Ed. 16). חמאה should be translated:
cream, not: *curd* (BDB), *butter* (Ges. Ed. 16.). אפר means:
ashes (BDB) not: *dust*. גור means: *lion cub* (BDB *whelp*),
not: *young lion* (Ges. Ed. 16.), which is: כפיר· צפור means:
birds (BDB), not: *winged creatures* (*Gefluegel* Ges. Ed. 16.).

The exact meanings should not be blurred by unnecessary
synonyms.[23] Thus in Ges. Ed. 16., אבל is translated both:
to complain and *to wail* (*klagen, jammern*), but should
properly be only: *to mourn* (*trauern*). טרף should not
mean: *to tear to pieces, to rob* (BDB, *tear, rend, pluck*),
but only: *to tear to pieces*. דמה should be translated:
to be like, not: *to be like, to be similar*, Ges. Ed. 16; *to be
like, resemble* (BDB). עיף means: *to be exhausted* (*er-
schoepft sein*) not: *to be fatigued, to be exhausted* (Ges.
Ed. 16); *to be faint, weary* (BDB). נתק means: *to tear off,
to tear loose*, not: *to cut off*.

Not only were the true meanings clouded by the use of
synonyms, but in Ges. Ed. 16. wrong meanings were often
added to correct ones.[24] קרח means: *ice*, not also: *hail.*
Ice is also the correct rendering in Ps. 147, 17 and Job 38, 29.
נבל means: *pitcher* (*Krug*), not also: *skin-bottle* (*Schlauch*,
Ges. Ed. 16.; BDB). אטר in Judges 3, 15, means: *to be
left-handed*, derived from: אטר *to bind*, Ps. 69, 16; lit., to
be closed as regards the right hand. Both meanings: *to be
crippled* and *one who uses both hands equally well*, which
Ges. Ed. 16 gave are incorrect. BDB correctly translated it:
a man *bound, restricted*, as to his right hand, i. e., *left-
handed.*

Some of these inexact and wrong meanings were due to a

---

[22] The references to Koenig's and Brown-Driver-Brigg's Lexicon are
ours.
[23] Delitzsch, Frd., *op. cit.*, 167 ff.
[24] *Ibidem*, 169.

careless use of the German, others were taken over directly from a like-sounding Arabic root. In Ges. Ed. 16., Delitzsch still found a strong Arabic influence,[25] which became pronounced from the Eighth Edition onwards. "Hebrew lexicography," said Delitzsch, "has been made the slave of the Arabic." [26] In his review of Ges. Ed. 9, in the *Prolegomena*, he had called attention to some of the instances in which the Arabic had been wrongly applied. Since then the fundamental meaning: *to be red*, from شقر for the Hebrew: שקר *to tell a falsehood*, had been dropped; also: *to break*, from the Arabic: فدر for: פדר *to be fat*. But Delitzsch showed that Ges. Ed. 16. still gave to Hebrew words meanings which were taken over from the Arabic. Thus: טל which only means: *dew*, received the additional meaning: *light-rain*, for the sake of the Arabic. גיא means: *valley;* for the sake of: جواء it received also the meaning: *lowland* (*Niederung*). ירט has the transitive meaning: *to deliver* (Ges. *preisgeben, zu freier Verfuegung hingeben*). For the sake of: ورط *to cast down*, the word is translated *to precipitate, deliver*. מוג means: *to melt*, then: *to dissolve, to be discouraged*. From the Arabic: موج *wave*, the word received the meanings: *to wave, to heave, to rock to and fro* (Ges. Ed. 16. *wogen, schwanken*). The entire root, as well as a hundred others, were dealt with in a wrong manner.[27] לאה should be translated: *to be powerless, to be unable*, a root that is found also in the Assyrian with this meaning. Ges. 16. preferred the secondary Arabic-Aramaic meaning: *to be tired, to lose courage* (BDB: *to be weary, impatient*), and developed the meaning: *to be unable*, by inserting the word: *fruitlessly; to be unable* was *to labor fruitlessly*. Quite naturally a wrong primary meaning upset all the developed meanings. Buhl in Ges. Ed. 16. did not always bear in mind that the Arabic often shows secondary meanings when compared with the older literary languages: Assyrian, Hebrew, and Aramaic.

Buhl, in Ges. Ed. 16. still treated as one root, words

---

[25] *Ibidem*, 171.
[26] *Ibidem*, 171.
[27] *Ibidem*, 173.

whose meanings show that they are homonymic roots in the
Hebrew.[28] פסח was translated: *to be lame, to limp*. From:
to hop over something, the meaning: *to leave untouched*
was developed. Brown-Driver-Briggs correctly distinguished two roots: I. *to spring over;* II. *to limp*. From:
כתר were developed both the meanings: *to surround* and:
to wait. The latter meaning was derived by saying: *to surround expectantly* (BDB. Ges. Ed. 16. *harrend umgeben*).
The root: זנח as the Assyrian: zinu: *to be angry* and the
Arab: زنخ *to stink*, show, should be divided, as was done
in BDB. Ges. Ed. 16. gave only one verb, with the primary meaning: *to stink*. Buhl derived the meaning: *to
reject*, by saying: *to spurn as loathesome*.

Whereas some roots should have been divided, others
should have been joined. טרף *prey*, for example, was
developed easily from the root: טרף *to tear to pieces*.
The general meaning: *food* was developed from: *prey*. Buhl
in Ges. Ed. 16. and Koenig refer the Hiphil, in Prov. 30, 8,
which is simply a denominative of: טרף to another root,
taken from the Arabic: ترف IV, *to grant good things*, following Barth.

Delitzsch goes on to show that the exegesis of the Bible
would derive benefit from a more thorough study of the
Hebrew usage. For example, he would translate the passage,
Prov. 14, 18: *The wise acquire knowledge*, instead of: *are
crowned with knowledge*, as Buhl, in Ges. Ed. 16. gave it.
The force of the words according to the grammar should
be brought out more exactly. For example, the Hithpael of:
דפק in Jud. 19, 22, should be translated: *to beat violently*
(BDB, *trommeln*), not merely: *to knock*, Ges. Ed. 16. Thus
many improvements are still in demand with regard to a
clearer expression of the Hebrew in German translation.

One of the chief difficulties that confronts the Hebrew
lexicographer, says Friedrich Delitzsch, is the corruption of
the Massoretic Text.[29] In the process of corruption two fac-
tors played a prominent part: (1) Matres lectiones were inserted often where they do not belong. (2) Many letters were
accidentally interchanged. Some of these are: ר and ד
ה and ת ; ו and י ; ד and נו-(ם)מ . A list of the different

---

[28] *Ibidem*, 192 f.
[29] *Ibidem*, 198 f.

kinds of corruption should be added to do away with the
unmethodical text-emendation. The lexicon is overloaded
with untenable emendations.

And finally Delitzsch advocated that the quoted examples
be given more in extenso, as was done in Latin and Greek
dictionaries. Words and constructions that occur in parallel passages should be cited as such. This would remove
the impression that all the citations are of equal value. For
it matters whether a construction is found in three or four
places, or actually only in one that has been repeated that
many times.

Although we might take exception to some of the details
of Delitzsch's criticism, it must be admitted that his general
criticism is correct. Buhl must be praised for the admirable
work which he bestowed upon this lexicon. Nevertheless
it must be admitted that Ges. Ed. 16. is not the finished
product which reviewers in general regarded it to be. It
excels in recording the different views of scholars on questions of exegesis, etymology, and text-criticism. It is deficient in lexicography proper. From the very beginning it
had been Gesenius' aim to determine the Hebrew meaning
from its own usage. He himself made some valuable contributions to this study. Buhl rescued the lexicon from the
disrepute into which it had fallen. But the task of the lexicographer is an enormous one, as the quotation from Scali-
ger on the fly-leaf of the lexicon indicates, and is still un-
finished.

The fact that a new revision of the lexicon has not been
undertaken for a decade is due, as so many other things, to
the exigencies of the World War. Upon the request of the
publishers, Buhl did not definitely resign as editor for a
new edition. Since the war, the publishers have declared
themselves against the publication of a new edition. The
price of the new lexicon for students would be prohibitive.
The publishers refused even to prepare the supplementary
pamphlet which Buhl advocated. In the meantime, theological students have set to work preparing glossaries for separate portions of the Old Testament. This, says Buhl, would
make the publishers even less inclined to prepare a new
edition. The edition which we have may therefore be
looked upon as the final one.[30]

---

[30] From a letter to me by Prof. Buhl, July 15, 1925.

CHAPTER VI

From the beginning Gesenius' influence on Hebrew lexicography extended beyond Germany, into Denmark, Sweden, and especially into England and America. His influence in the latter countries was most profound. We shall therefore devote this final chapter to a discussion of the most important lexicons that appeared in English, and were either based on or translated from Gesenius' lexicons.

As early as 1824, J. W. Gibbs, of Andover, prepared a translation of Gesenius' lexicon.[1] The basis of this translation was the abridgment of 1815. The larger work was constantly consulted, and additions were made from it. Corrections were also made from the *Lehrgebaeude,* 1817, and Gesenius' commentary on Isaiah, 1820-21. Rarely did the translator differ from the author or make a correction of his own. The 1827 and 1832 editions of this work are much smaller in size, less than one-half as thick as the first edition. The material in the lexicon was much abbreviated. The lexicon contained little more than the Hebrew words and their meanings. Most meanings were supported by only one citation, and the phrases and constructions found in the previous edition were almost all removed, as were the references to the cognate languages and the old versions.

Christopher Leo's translation of the first lexicon that had left Gesenius' hands, appeared a little later.[2] This lexicon, which appeared in two parts, formed a pretentious quarto volume when finished. The translation was made as literal as possible. Leo corrected some of Gesenius' citations and

---

[1] *A Hebrew and English Lexicon of the Old Testament, Including the Biblical Chaldee* . . . Andover, 1824; Edit. 2, London, 1828; Edit. 3, 1832.
[2] *A Hebrew Lexicon to the Books of the Old Testament, Including the Geographical Names and Chaldaic Words in Daniel, Esra, etc.* By Wilhelm Gesenius, 1824-28.

quotations. In some articles he made additions, e. g., he added passages in the articles: אָב - אָבֶן - אוֹר - אָדָם in order to elucidate Gesenius' meaning better. Whenever Gesenius differed from other lexicographers in the derivation of words, Leo tried to take note of it. He also added suggestions of his own. In the course of translation the shorter manual was published, and Leo made use of the corrections and additions which it contained. His lexicon was therefore an embodiment of the two editions. He included the valuable introduction and the analytical index. Gibbs had omitted both of these in his lexicon, but he had supplied a very good preface of his own. Leo's translation did not enjoy the popularity which Gibb's received. For students the volume was probably too ponderous, and the price, prohibitive. Moreover, the lexicon was based on Gesenius' juvenile production which was soon after superseded by his own revisions.

To make his work available to foreign students, Gesenius had published his Latin Manual.[3] Many of these were bought by American students. E. Robinson made the Latin lexicon of 1833 the basis of an English translation.[4]

Of Robinson's first edition, published in 1836, three thousand copies were sold at the end of three years, and a new edition became necessary. For this Gesenius had proposed to send his own corrections, which he had made for a new edition of his Manual Lexicon. In April, 1842, Gesenius sent a transcript of his own copy for a new edition of his own lexicon, which contained material as far as the letter: ח. He died before he could finish the rest of the manuscript. The notes which he left behind consisted only of short hints and references which he had intended to work out later. However, the part of the manuscript which Robinson had received from Gesenius was the most important, since it covered the part of the Manual which was most in need of correction. It contained roughly what was in the first two fasciculi of the Thesaurus which had been published in 1827 and 1835, and were now in need of revision. The

[3] *Lexicon Manuale Hebraicum et Chaldaicum in Veteris Testamenti Libros. Post Editionem Germanicam Tertiam Latine Elaboravit*, 1833; Edit. 2, by Hoffman, 1847.
[4] *A Hebrew and English Lexicon of the Old Testament, Including the Biblical Chaldee. From the Latin of Wm. Gesenius*, 1836.

remainder of the articles Robinson conformed to the Thesaurus as far as it had appeared. Only one more fasciculus
of the lexicographical material of the Thesaurus had to be
published. The second edition of Robinson's lexicon appeared in 1844. This edition was a decided improvement
upon the first. The publisher also improved the quality of
the type, and the printing was more correct. The third,
fourth and fifth editions appeared without the aid of the
concluding fasciculus of the Thesaurus. Robinson had made
arrangements with the publishers in Germany to insure
him of the reception of the concluding sheets, as soon as
they should come from the press. But the printing was
delayed.

In all these editions, Robinson allowed himself few additions of his own. Where he did add something, he put it in
brackets, with his signature. In 1853 the concluding fasciculus of the Thesaurus finally appeared. On the basis of this
Robinson corrected his translation. The material affected
was in the articles of those words which followed the root:
שבר in the Thesaurus. Many of the derivatives found a
place under: מ in Robinson's translation. In his section
of the Thesaurus, Roediger retained the leading features of
Gesenius' work, but the tone of his investigations was more
philosophical, and the comparisons with the Indo-Germanic
were eliminated altogether. The last edition which Robinson edited was the sixth, 1855. It exhibits a summary of
the latest labors of Gesenius in the field of Hebrew lexicography.

Robinson rendered a noteworthy service to the study of
Hebrew by translating Gesenius' lexicon, even if his own
contributions were meagre. The lexicon was in use much
longer than it deserved to be. The fact that it is still in
print, the most recent impression we have seen being the
thirty-fourth, from rather worn plates, attests its need and
its popularity. Although it contains much that is still of
value, its etymological and comparative sections are sadly
deficient.

The next English Gesenius to put in its appearance was
edited by S. P. Tregelles, a scholar better known for his
excellent work in connection with the Greek text of the New
Testament. He published his translation in England, in

1846.[5] This translation was begun to supplant Gibb's translation, which was then out of print, and really too inade-
quate to be reprinted. The first edition of Robinson's lexicon was hard to obtain. Besides, Tregelles held that this
translation showed much haste and oversight, as it actually
did; and Robinson had made no comment whatever with
regard to Gesenius' rationalistic interpretations in theological articles. Meanwhile Robinson's second edition was issued. Tregelles considered it to be much better than the
first; however, since Robinson had again made no comments
on the theological views of Gesenius, and had allowed himself to make other alterations and omissions, with which
Tregelles did not agree, the latter went ahead with the
publication of his edition.

For the preparation of his lexicon, Tregelles used the
Lexicon Manualis, of 1833, as Robinson had done, and he
compared it with the Thesaurus. In the course of time,
Hoffmann's edition of the Latin Manual appeared, and Tregelles made use of that, together with the part of the Thesaurus that had been completed by Roediger. He verified
the Scripture references and made such corrections as he
thought needful. He compared every word with Lee's[5a]
Hebrew Lexicon; and when statements of Gesenius were
questioned he consulted the best authorities to be had at
that time in Arabic and Hebrew, and added his own opinions in brackets. He availed himself of Robinson's translation as well as of his *Biblical Researches*.

Tregelles allowed himself great freedom in correcting
Gesenius' rationalistic views. He wanted to query every
statement "in which doubt is cast upon Scripture inspira-
tion, or in which the New and Old Testament are spoken of
as discrepant, or in which mistakes and ignorance are
charged upon the 'Holy men of God who wrote as they
were moved by the Holy Ghost.'" A few illustrations will
suffice. Concerning: עִמָּנוּאֵל.[6] Gesenius had said in his Thes.,
1044, and in both editions of his Latin Manual: *nomen sym-*

[5] *Gesenius' Hebrew and Chaldee Lexicon to the Old Testament Scriptures. Translated with Additions and Corrections from the Author's
Thesaurus and Other Works*. . . 1846.
[5a] *A Lexicon Hebrew, Chaldee, and English*, 1840, 1844. London.
[6] It is to be noted that both Robinson and Dietrich who intended to
preserve Gesenius' view altered it here. Robinson pruned off the
objectionable feature and said: "The symbolical and prophetical name
of a child."

bolicum et propheticum filii Jesaiae prophetae, Jes. VII, 14; VII, 8. Tragelles reproduced this and added: "This is utterly false, it is the name of the son who should be born of the Virgin, and it designates Him as being truly 'God over all blessed forever,' Isa. 7, 14; 8, 8." In the article עלמה which Robinson, 1854, following Gesenius' latest view[7] rendered: "a bride, a youthful spouse, a wife recently married, Isa., 7, 14," Tregelles refers to the rendering in the LXX; the use of the word Alma in Punic, which means Virgin according to a tradition preserved in Jerome; and then he appealed to the absolute authority of the New Testament to settle the question for a Christian.

Tregelles also made other changes. He often made a different selection of material from Gesenius' Thesaurus than Robinson had done and added more materials of his own. For instance, Robinson gave only one root: ספח following Gesenius. Tregelles distinguished two: I. only in Niphal, *to be added;* II. *to pour.* In his article Robinson made no attempt to show how the meaning: *to adjoin oneself* had been developed from the primary meaning: *to pour out.* Likewise: נחל which Robinson, 1854, had treated as one root, was divided into two by Tregelles: I. *to receive;* and II. *to flow,* the latter found in derivations only.

The translation of Tregelles was excellent in many respects, and it enjoyed a great popularity. In 1857, another edition was issued. The latest edition which we have seen was printed in 1890.

The most recent, as well as the best translation based on Gesenius' lexicographical labors is the so-called Oxford Hebrew Lexicon, prepared by Brown, Driver, and Briggs. The preparation of this lexicon extended over a period of twenty-three years. The first part was issued in 1892. The lexicon appeared complete, in 1906, as: *A Hebrew and Eng-*

---

[7] In his first two editions, Gesenius had said that this word meant: a virgin, always unmarried and mature. From Gesenius 3. on he said that the stress is on the maturity not the virginity, although marriage is usually excluded. He considered the LXX rendition in Isa. 7, 14: παρθενος to be incorrect. In his Thesaurus he weakened his latter statement when he added that both: בתולה and παρθενος were sometimes used to stress maturity, and not virginity. Buhl in Ges. Ed. 16. put the stress on: maturity, and made no comment concerning the Greek translation, while Koenig, in his latest edition, states that the LXX translation in Isa. 7, 14 is not "in reality wrong" (Edit. 3, 331). So far as we know, the word never meant "young married woman". Cf. Wilson, *Princeton Theo. Review,* XXIV, 316.

lish Lexicon of the Old Testament. Nominally based on Robinson's translation, this is almost an entirely new work both as to material as well as to arrangement. Since its preparation extended over the period of time which was required for the publication of the eleventh to the fourteenth editions of the German Gesenius, the editors could avail themselves of their materials. Ges. Ed. 14. was not published until the Oxford Lexicon was in type, with the exception of the appendix, and could therefore not be of much use to the editors.

The division of the work was as follows: Driver wrote all the articles on the particles, including such words as were originally nouns, but whose principal use is adverbial; also entire stems whose one derivation only is adverbial. Besides these he prepared other articles. Briggs prepared the articles important to Old Testament religion, theology, and psychology, and words related to these. Brown was responsible for all the remaining articles, and supervised the general arrangement and oversight of the work. Each article was thoroughly revised, so that this dictionary was really an entirely new work.

A complete revision was necessitated by the fact that the words of the lexicon were not arranged alphabetically, but according to their roots. Gesenius had used the alphabetical arrangement in his Thesaurus, but so far it had not been introduced in his Manual Lexicon. Siegfried, who reviewed the first part of this Oxford Lexicon,[8] considered this arrangement premature. Barth's and De Lagarde's works on the formation of Hebrew nouns had shown too many difficulties still obtaining in the study of the roots of Hebrew nouns. Noeldeke had warned against any premature foreclosures in this matter. Eduard Koenig, on the other hand, welcomed this arrangement.[9] Both Kimchi and Buxtorf had believed it to be the most practicable scheme, and had used it for their lexicons.

The alphabetical arrangement may be the more scientific, but it presents difficulties, as Siegfried showed.[10] He cited a number of examples from the first letter of the alphabet only, which showed the uncertainty still prevailing with re-

---

[8] *Theo. Literaturzeitung,* 1892, 101 f.
[9] *Theo. Literaturblatt,* 1896, 148.
[10] *Op. cit.,* 102.

gard to certain roots. The word: אָב was derived from
the root: אָבה II. At the same time the editors spoke just
as convincingly of the view that it is a primitive noun,
emanating from the nursery. אָב was derived from: אבב
but a reference has to be made to the root: אנב also.
אִיוּב was derived from the root: אִיב, yet in the article the
editors must admit that all is uncertain with regard to this
root. אֵל and אֱלהים were derived from the root: אלה
nevertheless we see that the root: אוּל has just as much for
it, when we read the article in which all the views are
brought together. The words: אָלֶה - אַלוֹן - אֵלה - אַלּוֹן were
derived from: אוּל and אֵלל II, derivations against which
Siegfried raised his objections. אִישׁ is derived from: אֵישׁ
and אוּשׁ according to Gesenius' Thesaurus; but the editors
admitted that these etymologies are uncertain, and devoted
a whole paragraph to the discussion of opposing views.
Examples of this kind could be added to Siegfried's in
great number from other parts of the lexicon. The alphabetical order may not be a great annoyance to scholars, but
students are surely hindered by it in the initial stages of
their studies. Words whose etymology was still uncertain
had to be listed also in their alphabetical order, and cross-
references became necessary. This consumed space, and a
very compact system of abbreviations had to be resorted to.
For example, in the article on Ephod, under 3a, we read:
"acc. to Thes. al plus St. Bu RS [115] -2b;Stu. Be Ry al regard
as sub 1." This means: "according to the Thesaurus of
Gesenius and others, according to Stade and Budde (Judges
and Samuel, p. 115) it means a gilded image; according to
Studer, Bertheau, Ryssel it is to be understood of a garment
of the priest." The abbreviations of the lexicon became
quite complicated.

The remarks which Friedrich Delitzsch made in connection with Ges. Ed. 16, applied also to this lexicon, as we
have seen. The editors were influenced by the Arabic in
the determination of primary meanings and their developments. These we have considered in connection with Delitzsch's review.

The editors increased their difficulties in etymology by
including the explanation and translation of proper-names.
They understood that they were undertaking a very difficult

task, and expected that exception would be taken to many
of their etymologies of proper-names.

In other respects the lexicon resembled Buhl's editions of
the lexicon. The Oxford Lexicon is especially rich in citations and quotations. The editors also attempted to give
an impartial resume of the different views held by scholars
in Old Testament studies. The Aramaic was separated from
the Hebrew lexicon proper and placed at the end of the
book. The plan to include also an English-Hebrew vocabulary had to be given up as the lexicon grew too large.

The different sections of the lexicon were favorably reviewed in Germany by scholars as Eduard Koenig[10a] and C.
Siegfried.[10b] The former praised the scholarship of the
editors very highly. He admired the learning and diligence
which they exercised in etymology, in the comparison of
the related languages, and in the archaeological, historical,
and Biblical-theological materials. He said that the lexicon
is remarkably complete and objective in its presentation of
the divergent views of scholars. Another feature that was
commended was the excellent print, and the comparative
freedom from errors in the text. The material was not so
crowded as in the edition Ges. Ed. 16. In aesthetic beauty
the lexicon surpasses any other Hebrew lexicon.

As Gesenius, Ed. 16., the edition by Brown, Driver and
Briggs is almost a Hebrew thesaurus. The statistical exact-
ness in recording the citations from the Hebrew language is,
of course, greater than in Gesenius' Thesaurus. For example, in Gesenius, the expression: הירדן הזה was omitted in
the article on: ירדן. This phrase is found in the lexicon by
Brown, Driver, and Briggs, and is important since it shows
that: ירדן was originally an appellative. The purely linguistical, comparative, geographical, and archaeological materials in the edition by Brown, Driver, and Briggs are
more accurate than those in the Thesaurus. Nevertheless, the
method in their lexicon is theoretical, that is, it is not one
of investigation, but simply a compilation of results. Gesenius' Thesaurus is still valuable for its detailed investigations and the excerpts which it contains from the writings

---

[10a] *Theo. Literaturzeitung*, Pt. I, 1893, 101 ff.; Pt. II-IV, 1896, 2 ff.
[10b] *Theo. Literaturblatt*, Pt. I-IV, 1896, 147 ff.; Pt. VI, 1898, 273 ff.

produced by men of Ancient Greece, Rome, and Arabia,
most of them translated, which could not, and should not
be taken into a manual lexicon.

In the course of time, Gesenius' lexicon became the out-
standing work in Hebrew lexicography, both in German
and in English. The lexicons of Fuerst, Siegfried, and
Eduard Koenig are also based more or less on Gesenius'
lexicon. And there are other Hebrew lexicons that owe
much to him. To Gesenius belongs the distinction of having begun a lexicon that maintained its supremacy for over
a hundred years. Now both the German and English editions are in need of revision. It is to be hoped that a new
revision may be undertaken, so that Gesenius' work may be
brought to ever greater completion.

BIBLIOGRAPHY

BIOGRAPHY: Gesenius, H. W., *Gesenius . . . Ein Erinnerungsblatt on den hundertjaehrigen Geburtstag am 3. Feb., 1886, Halle, 1886.* (Contains obituary notices from: *Intelligenzblatt der Allgemeinen Literaturzeitung,* 1842, 505 ff. [no author]); Fritzsche, W. *Gesenius, Das Hallische Patriotische Wochenblatt,* Nov. 5, 1842; *Die Leipziger Allgemeine Zeitung,* Nov. 1, 1842 (no author).)

Neuer Nekrolog der Deutschen, 1842, II, 737 ff. (used the above-mentioned material).

Redslob, *Allgemeine deutsche Biographia,* IX, 89 f.

Kraetzschmar R. (Reuss, E.), W. *Gesenius, Realencyclopaedie fuer protestantische Theologie u. Kirche,* 3. Ed., VI, 624 f.

Robinson, E., *Notices of Gesenius, Bibliotheca Sacra,* 1843, 361 ff.

Cheyne, *Founders of Old Testament Criticism,* 1893.

IMPORTANT PRECURSORS OF GESENIUS:

Coccejus, L., *Lexicon et Commentarius . . .* Ed. II, Majus, 1689.

Schultens, A., *Liber Jobi . . .* Leyden, 2 Vol., 1737.

Schultens, A., *Origines Hebraeae . . .* Leyden, 1761.

Michaelis, J. D., *Supplementa ad Lexica Hebraeica,* Goettingen, 2 Vols., 1792.

Simonis, J., *Lexicon Manuale Hebraeicum et Chaldaeicum,* Halle, 1752; Ed. II, 1771; Ed. III, by J. G. Eichhorn, 1793; Ed. IV, Winer, 1824.

GESENIUS, HEBREW LEXICONS, SOME REVIEWS, AND TRANSLATIONS.

Gesenius, W., *Hebraeisch-deutsches Handwoerterbuch ueber die Schriften des Alten Testaments,* 1810-1812.

REVIEWS: Part I, *Allegemeine Literaturzeitung,* 1810, 809 ff.; Part II, *ibid.,* 1812, 169 ff.

TRANSLATION: Leo, C., *A Hebrew Lexicon to the Books of the Old Testament, Cambridge,* 1825-1828.

Gesenius, W., *Neues hebraeisch-deutsches Handwoerterbuch ueber das Alte Testament mit Einschluss des biblischen Chaldaeismus. Ein Auszug aus dem groesseren Werke,* Leipzig, 1815.

REVIEW: *.Allgemeine Literaturzeitung,* 1815, 449 ff.

TRANSLATION: Gibbs, J. W., *A Hebrew and English Lexicon, Including the Biblical Chaldee,* Andover, 1824; London, 1828, 1832. Ed. II bears the title: *A Manual Hebrew and English Lexicon, Including the Biblical Chaldee.*

Gesenius, W., *Hebraeisches und chaldaeisches Handwoerterbuch . . .* Zweite Auflage, 1823.

REVIEW: *Goettinger Gelehrten Anzeigen,* 1824, 1012 ff.

Gesenius, W., *Hebraeisches und chaldaeisches Handwoerterbuch.* . .
Dritte Auflage, 1828.

REVIEW: Faesi, *Neue Jahrbuecher fuer Philologie und Paedagogik,* IV,
Hft. I, 1832, 155 ff.

Gesenius, W., *Thesaurus Philologicus criticus linguae Hebraeae et
Chaldaeae Veteris Testamenti. Ed. altera secundum radices digesta
germanica longe auctior et emendatior,* 1829-1858. (Roediger furnished
the two fasciculi completed after Gesenius' death, in 1853 and 1858.)

REVIEW: *Allgmeine Literaturzeitung,* 1841, 305 ff.

Gesenius, W., *Lexicon Manuale Hebraeicum et Chaldaeicum in Veteris
Testamenti libros post editionem germanicam tertiam.* . . 1833. Review:
Allgemeine Literaturzeitung, 1834, 305 ff.

TRANSLATIONS: Robinson, E. *A Hebrew and English Lexicon of the
Old Testament* . . . *From the Latin of William Gesenius.* Boston, 1836,
1844, 1849, 1850, 1854.

Tregelles, S. P., *Gesenius' Hebrew and Chaldee Lexicon to the Old
Testament Scriptures.* . . London, 1846; 2 Ed. 1857.

Gesenius, W., *Hebraeisches und chaldaeisches Handwoerterbuch ueber
das Alte Testament,* 1834. Vierte Ausgabe.

Dietrich, F. F. C., *Hebraeisches und chaldaeisches Handwoerterbuch.*
Von Wilhelm Gesenius.

5. Aufl. 1857; 6. 1863; 7. 1868.

Muehlau and Volck, *Wilhelm Gesenius' Hebraeisches und chaldaeisches
Handwoerterbuch ueber das Alte Testament.* 8. Ed. 1878; 9. Ed. 1883.

REVIEWS: Ed. 8, Kautzsch, *Theo. Literaturzeitung,* 1878, 433 f. Ed. 9,
Siegfried, *Theo. Literaturzeitung,* 1883, 529.

Noeldeke, Th., *ZDMG,* 1886, 718, refers to 8. 9. 10. Eds.

De Lagarde, *Goettinger G. A.,* 1884, 287-288.

Muehlau, F., and Volck, W., *Wilhelm Gesenius' Hebraeisches u. Aramaeisches Handwoerterbuch ueber das Alte Testament,* 10. Ed.. *Mit Bei-
traegen von Dr. D. H. Mueller,* 1886; 11. Ed. 1890.

Buhl, Fr., *Wilhelm Gesenius' Hebraeisches u. Aramaeisches Handwoerterbuch ueber das Alte Testament, in Verbindung mit Prof. Albert
Socin u. Prof. H. Zimmern.* 12 Ed. 1895.

REVIEWS: Bevan, A., *Critical Review,* 1895, 128 ff. Siegfried, C.,
Theo. Literaturzeitung, 1895, 302 ff. Strack, H., *Theo. Literaturblatt,*
1895, 385 ff., Ed. 13, published in 1899.

REVIEWS: Perles, F., *Jewish Quarterly Review,* 1899, 688 ff. Schwally,
F., *Theo. Literaturzeitung,* 1899, 355 ff. R. Z., *Theo. Literaturblatt,*
1900, 52 ff.

Buhl, F., *Wilhelm Gesenius' Hebraeisches u. Aramaeisches Handwoerterbuch ueber das Alte Testament. In Verbindung mit H. Zimmern.*
14. Ed., 1905.

REVIEWS: Perles, F., *JQR,* 1906, 383 ff.; Schwally, Fr., *Theo. Literaturzeitung,* 1905, 611 ff. ; Koenig, E., *Theo. Literaturblatt,* 1905, 449 ff.

Brown, Driver, Briggs, *A Hebrew and English Lexicon of the Old
Testament* . . . *Based on the Lexicon of W. Gesenius as Translated by
Edward Robinson,* Cambridge, 1906. (P. I. was ready in 1892).

REVIEWS: Siegfried, C., Part I, *Theo. Literaturzeitung,* 1893, 101 ff.;
Siegfried, Part II-IV, *ibid,* 1896, 2 ff.

Koenig, E., P. I-IV, *Theo Literaturblatt,* 1896, 147 ff. Koenig, P. VI,
ibid., 1898, 273 ff.

Buhl, F., *Wilhelm Gesenius' Hebraeisches u. Aramaeisches Handwoerterbuch ueber das Alte Testament.* In Verbindung mit H. Zimmern,
W. Max Mueller, und O. Weber bearbeitet. Ed. 16., 1915.

REVIEWS: Schwally, Fr., *Theo. Literaturzeitung,* 1916, 26 ff. Cas-
pari, W., *Theo. Literaturblatt,* 1915, 488 f.; Delitzsch, Fr., *Philologische
Forderungen an die hebraeische Lexikographie,* 1916, 160 ff. and 192 ff.,
Orientalistische Literaturzeitung.

Edition 17, published in Leipzig, 1921, is an anastatic reprint of the 16.
Other lexicons and books that show the influence of Gesenius on Hebrew lexicography.

Fuerst, J., *Hebraeisches und Chaldaeisches Handwoerterbuch ueber das Alte Testament* . . . Leipzig, 1857; Ed. 2. 1863; Ed. 3, by V. Ryssel, 1876; Davidson, S., made an English translation ,New York, 1867.

Siegfried, C. and Stade, B., *Hebraeisches Woerterbuch zum Alten Testament*, 1892-1893.

Review: Budde, K., *Theo. Literaturzeitung*, 1892, 58 ff. and 1894, 415 ff.

Levy, J. L., *Neuhebraeisches u. chaldaeisches Woerterbuch ueber die Talmudim u. Midraschim*, 1879.

Koenig, F., *Hebraeisches u. Aramaeisches Woerterbuch* . . . Leipzig, 1910; 2. and 3. Edit, 1922.

Gesenius, W., *Hebraeische Grammatik*, 1813.

Gesenius, W., *Geschichte der hebraeischen Sprache u. Schrift*, 1815.

Gesenius, W., *Philologisch-kritischer u. historischer Commentar ueber den Jesaia.* . . 1820-1821; 2. Ed. contains translation only, 1829.

Ewald, H., *Kritische Grammatik der Hebraeischen Sprache*, 1827.

Delitzsch, Fried, *The Hebrew Language Viewed in the Light of Assyrian Research*, 1883.

Bleek, J., and Kamphausen, A., *Einleitung in das Alte Testament*, von Fr. Bleek, 1865, p. 138 ff.